NOT *without* God

Praises for *Not Without God*

Zina's story is a fascinating story of faith, perseverance, and determination. She is an ongoing testimony of the power of God to walk with us through the most difficult situations and to bring us to a place of triumph. Zina shows us all that regardless of what happens to us, we don't have to be victims. We can find victory in our weaknesses and hope in our suffering. Her undying faith, her authenticity about her struggles, and her gift of encouragement inspires all who know her and her story.

—**Sharon Gibson**, Creator of the
"How to Write for Fun and Profit" online course
and author of *From Stuck to Success*

Not Without God is an inspiring true story of courage, perseverance, and faith. Written with heart and spirit, it chronicles Zina's amazing journey of healing filled with examples of strength, boldness, and miracles. Her story will bring you to tears and leave you inspired to never give up, dominate over your fears, take the risks worth taking, step out in faith, and start living your vision. Her story is a powerful reminder of what is truly most important in life: faith, hope and love.

—**Millie Chu**, Business professor and founder of
A2 Leap non-profit organization

NOT *without* God

a story of
SURVIVAL

Zina Hermez

NEW YORK

NOT *without* **God**
a story of SURVIVAL

© 2015 **Zina Hermez**.

Published in New York, New York, by Morgan James Publishing. Morgan James and The Entrepreneurial Publisher are trademarks of Morgan James, LLC.
www.MorganJamesPublishing.com

The Morgan James Speakers Group can bring authors to your live event. For more information or to book an event visit The Morgan James Speakers Group at www.TheMorganJamesSpeakersGroup.com.

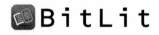

**A FREE eBook edition is available
with the purchase of this print book**

CLEARLY PRINT YOUR NAME IN THE BOX ABOVE

Instructions to claim your free eBook edition:
1. Download the BitLit app for Android or iOS
2. Write your name in UPPER CASE in the box
3. Use the BitLit app to submit a photo
4. Download your eBook to any device

ISBN 978-1-63047-127-9 paperback
ISBN 978-1-63047-128-6 eBook
ISBN 978-1-63047-129-3 hardcover
Library of Congress Control Number:
2014933859

Cover Design by:
Rachel Lopez
www.r2cdesign.com

Interior Design by:
Bonnie Bushman
bonnie@caboodlegraphics.com

In an effort to support local communities, raise awareness and funds, Morgan James Publishing donates a percentage of all book sales for the life of each book to Habitat for Humanity Peninsula and Greater Williamsburg.

Get involved today, visit
www.MorganJamesBuilds.com.

**Habitat
for Humanity®**
Peninsula and
Greater Williamsburg
Building Partner

To my holy Father God and His only Son, my Lord and Savior Jesus Christ, for saving my life and bringing me through many troubled waters…Lord, "I shall not want" (Psalm 23:1).

My prayer is that this is written in such a way that all who read my words are able to get insight into how to heal from their own suffering of any kind, through my example. That maybe they can deal with their issues and be inspired through my hard work and tireless faith. Most of all, I pray that they see You, Lord, and Your love for me—how You always help me and how You can help them too, every day.

Contents

Acknowledgments ix

Prologue xi

Chapter 1   The Crash   1

Chapter 2   Heaven on Earth—in a Hospital   14

Chapter 3   Life after the Accident: 33
Facing the Great Unknown

Chapter 4   Physical Therapy—My Progression   50
and Recovery

Chapter 5   Some Quick Tips on How I Heal   67

Chapter 6   "Faith of a Million Dollars!"   77

Chapter 7   Going Out into the Real World   87

Chapter 8   Prepared for a Purpose   101

Chapter 9   Where I Am Now   110

About the Author   119

Appendix 1   What Do the Doctors Say?   120

Appendix 2   Startling Facts about Spinal Cord Injury   125

Acknowledgments

All my life the Lord has sent the right people at the right moments to give me encouragement and offer hope. In tragedy, they have even saved my life. They are doctors, nurses, teachers, and friends. I've been blessed to have a lot of good people supporting me. I want to thank all of them.

To everyone who saved my life at the University of Michigan C.S. Mott Children's Hospital, in the first hours after my accident to the first several weeks—words cannot express the gratitude I feel in my heart. Thank you.

I would like to thank everyone who made this book possible for me. David Hancock, Rick Frishman, Terry Whalin, Amanda Rooker, Angie Kiesling, and everyone at the Morgan James Publishing team for believing in me and for your support. It means so much. Thank you.

I would like to thank my parents and siblings for never giving up on the hope for my recovery. And to my awesome nieces and nephews, whose youth kept me young and laughing. I love you all.

To the many students and friends I've made throughout the years. God bless you…

Prologue

As a child I knew my path would not be easy. God would tell me, not always in language, but in feelings and thoughts. God doesn't only use words to communicate. He was preparing me for what was to come. He assured me I would get through it. I felt His presence; I knew there was a God and that He was mighty.

From a very young age I used to question my existence. I was a deep thinker. I had premonitions. I felt different. Before my accident I would ask God to make me a better person. Confused by the crowd I hung out with at school, and by my surroundings, I knew the things others deemed as important such as money and status didn't mean much in the larger scheme of life. I wanted to understand more. I knew there was a true love beyond what I witnessed, but I didn't know how to grasp it.

I chose to call this book *Not without God: A Story of Survival* to describe how I never could have survived my accident without the Lord. I realize this title has double meaning. When I state "Not without God" it also means I have never lived without Him, not only in my *Story of Survival* but even in times when I didn't realize He was there. As an adult I clearly see that I have never been *without God.* This title encompasses my life.

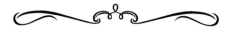

Chapter 1

The Crash

"They're getting you help!" a woman said. "Hold on, Zina, we're almost there. Oh, Zina, hold on."

The noise from the rotor told me I was on a helicopter. Fading in and out each time she gently rubbed my shoulder, I fought to stay awake.

"I'm Mary Kay," she said, "the University of Michigan Survival Life Flight nurse." I squinted into fathomless light blue eyes, like an ocean. To me she was an angel. "We're taking you to U of M. They'll take good care of you there, Zina. Hold on, Zina, hold on."

In my sixteen short years, I'd never heard such compassion. I held onto her voice and fought to stay alive. I had never flown and was more afraid of the height than of my injuries. I knew the Lord was with me.

I could not move or talk—just mumble. I couldn't comprehend what had happened, but I knew I'd been hurt, badly. Mary Kay's voice was my lifeline. Hold on, Zina, hold on.

Who would've thought I would be fighting for my life? I had just been trying to get to school.

Somehow I felt a peace I cannot explain. I was hurt and I needed love badly. It was as if Mary Kay felt all my pain, and all I could do was wait and hope my life would be spared.

A Fateful Day

On a brisk day in September 1994, still early in the school year, Mr. Peolke knocked on our classroom door. "Can I have a word with Zina?" he asked my teacher. Sure I had done something wrong, I squirmed in my chair. When a vice-principal comes to visit you, it usually isn't for a good reason. Of course, my teacher agreed. Reluctantly I slid out of my desk and approached him, stepping into the hallway to meet him outside. *What have I done now?*

He leaned forward to reach me at eye level in his nice distinguished suit. *Oh no, I'm in trouble, here it comes.* To my surprise, I was not.

"Zina, I'd like you to represent Harrison High School on the Multicultural/Multiracial Community Council this year," he said in a kind and gentle tone. "Are you interested?" The council was a diversity panel being implemented for the first time that would include schools in our district.

I wasn't expecting that. *Why would he choose me?* I didn't feel worthy. "Uh, yeah, of course, Mr. Peolke, thank you!" I replied.

Following a series of afterschool meetings, a large assembly was to be held in our gym with teachers and students. The whole school would be there.

Unfortunately, I never fulfilled my service on the council that year, nor was I able to make it to the assembly. My accident happened on October 18, 1994, just a little over a month into the school year.

I tried my best to live a normal teenage life—until that dark rainy October morning when everything changed. I woke up late for school. The bus that came in front of my house to pick me up had already passed.

When I missed my bus that year I would walk down to my best friend's house. His bus came a little later at around 7:10, so this bought me more time if I was running late.

I felt relieved, like a ton of weights had been lifted off me because I could still get to school on time and make it to my after-school council meetings.

On my way to my best friend's house I had to cross a busy two-lane road. Even though it was just a few minutes after seven, the drizzle in the dark made it seem like the middle of the night.

The traffic was heavy and seemed never to end. I stood there waiting to cross, not knowing I was awaiting my fate. I must've thought I had clearance because I crossed. I was in trouble. The woman traveling south, Theresa, didn't see me. On her way to work, going 50 mph in a 30 mph school zone, she was driving too fast.

A man named Robert was driving the second car behind her. He saw her swerve to the right, but he couldn't understand why until he saw me lying on the ground. He grabbed a blanket from his car and waited with me until the ambulance came. The driver immediately behind him ran to my neighbor's house and banged on their door for them to call 911.

In a split second my future became unpredictable, grim.

My mother heard Theresa's screams from her bedroom. She and my dad and two sisters came running out. My dad ran up to me, but when the ambulance got there the paramedics, police, and firemen didn't let my family near me, not even to ride in the ambulance. My sister later told me that when they first came out several people were already helping me. Of course my family was hysterical—as was Theresa. I needed medical attention fast.

My abdomen eviscerated from the crash, exposing some of my organs. I had an extended flap-like opening from the middle of my stomach to the mid portion of my upper back, and blood was gushing out. My spine shifted and broke at the lumbar level. I had a fracture in my first cervical vertebrae. My lower legs were "deformed" and I could not move them. My ribs were broken. I had extensive internal bleeding and a broken femur on the left. The bones of both lower legs were broken as well. I'm lucky it wasn't worse.

But with all those injuries, I was never unconscious for any length of time. I faded in and out, mumbling, not making much sense, but I was able to follow simple commands.

The ambulance took me to Botsford, a local hospital in Michigan, but I had to be airlifted to the University of Michigan hospital via helicopter because they are a level-one trauma hospital. That was where I met Mary Kay and the others from the Survival Life Flight team. A Botsford Hospital physician told my family that my condition was critical and I may not make it. If I did, the likelihood of a lower spinal injury was very high. I don't recall Botsford Hospital because I was there just under an hour.

The next thing I remembered was my body being lifted. Within twenty minutes the University of Michigan Survival Life Flight crew arrived. I was given two units of blood in the emergency room while they stabilized my spine. They also inserted a breathing tube and gave me medication to numb me as they prepped me for the helicopter ride.

When I arrived at U of M I immediately went into twelve hours of emergency surgery. The exploration of my abdomen revealed no injury to my stomach. My abdominal wall was closed, and orthopedic surgeons inserted rods and screws to hold my broken lower-leg bones in place. They also reset my left femur fracture and performed bilateral fasciotomies.

A fasciotomy is a surgical procedure where the fascia is cut to relieve tension or pressure (and treat the resulting loss of circulation to an area of tissue or muscle). The *fascia* is connective tissue that surrounds muscles, groups of muscles, blood vessels, and nerves, binding those structures together. It's like a plastic wrap that can be used to hold the contents of a sandwich together. A fasciotomy is a limb-saving procedure. I have two fasciotomy scars below my knees on the inside of my shins. God not only saved my life and shielded my head from injury, He saved my limbs.

I didn't have a near-death experience. I didn't see white pearly gates. Jesus didn't carry me to heaven. In bestsellers such as *90 Minutes in Heaven* by Don Piper and Cecil Murphy, or *Heaven Is for Real* by Todd Burpo and Lynn Vincent, the main characters make a trip to heaven and back.

I've asked God why I never got to see heaven. The only answer I received is, *"Because you would not have come back. And I couldn't do that to you. I couldn't let you see heaven and then send you back."* In *Heaven Is for Real* Jesus explains to Colton, a little boy, why he has to come back. Jesus says He is answering Colton's dad's prayer. In *90 Minutes in Heaven*, Don Piper describes how he understood it was time to come back. But if I saw God I would not want to come back. After all, I didn't have much to come back to.

Growing Up on "Gratitude" Court

Our house was on a dead-end street named Gramercy Court that consisted of eighteen homes. It was the first house on the left when you made a right turn onto Gramercy while going south. I used to take my bike and ride up and down our street for what seemed like hours, riding onto the circle where there was grass and a large tree I liked to climb. Evening would set in and still I rode, feeling the wind in my face as I pedaled up and down our street.

I also used to stand in our front yard or on the side of the house and water the trees and grass and plants in the summer—for a long time. My mom would call me in and say "What are you doing?" with a funny look on her face. What I was doing didn't seem normal, I suppose, but at eight, nine, ten years old I really felt I was doing justice to that grass and those trees by watering them. It was hot out, and I wanted to cool the plants.

My brothers and sisters always laughed at me for spending so much time watering the trees and plants. There was one tree in particular I used to water a lot on the side of our house.

Growing up, the name "Gramercy" always meant something to me but I couldn't understand why. Eventually I looked up the word *gramercy* and found that it means "gratitude" or "many thanks." I'm thankful to be alive so now I know why.

I lived in what seemed to be a *Leave It to Beaver* type neighborhood, but I didn't have the best of childhoods. My crowd of friends was superficial at best. Confused by my surroundings, I knew the people who inhabited my space were not entirely living their faith, but I didn't completely know what that meant or how to do so myself. I knew there was something greater than what I could see.

Each night I'd pray in bed before I fell asleep, asking God to make me a better person. *I don't get it, God. But I want to know You. I don't completely understand but I want to. Help me.* Things were hard at home. My family fought often and my parents had a busy social life that took them out of the home on frequent occasions. A loner by nature, I covered my teenage angst by staying busy, hanging out with friends here and there, and seeking solitude whenever I needed to focus inward. It's difficult to see God in those situations or believe that a loving God would allow you to suffer. When we are in pain we may doubt that there even is a God. Nevertheless, I always felt His presence with me and knew He was there. So I would talk to Him at night, asking Him to help me be a good person.

I never dreamed the answer to that prayer would come through tragedy.

Whispers from God

As a child, I would escape to quietness. Daily in the summer I would go outside to ride my ten-speed bike until the sun went down. Most of my neighbors were indoors for dinner during these times. But as nighttime drew closer, even in the dusk, I wanted to stay outside.

On these evening rides I would hear from God. *"This path will not be easy,"* He often told me. *"But I will never leave you nor forsake you."* I pedaled faster, my heart thrumming. What did it all mean? One thing I knew for sure: He would always be with me.

Often I would hear the sound of clinking silverware through my neighbors' screen doors as they talked about their workday and shared the evening meal with their families. I don't know what I enjoyed more—the peaceful ride on these summer evenings or observing these upper-middle-class families. There were lessons to be learned. Their normalcy, I observed.

Mr. Kahl, our next-door neighbor, spent a lot of time working outside in his yard. With his tools on his belt, he worked tirelessly on his garden and flowers and cut the grass almost daily. His grass was greener than any I had ever seen. Excited, I'd wave every time I saw him.

"Well, hello there, Zina," he would say in a genuine tone. He was my favorite neighbor and inspired me to water the grass and flowerbeds in my own yard. These opportunities to say hello while neighbors were outside made me wonder what it was like in their houses. I wondered if it was anything like mine.

I may have been young. I may have been a girl. But I felt this connection to some of my neighbors I could not explain. I especially liked the quietness of those rides, the peace. The silence made it easier to feel the presence of God and know He was there. As a child, it was the only way to escape to my own little silent retreat—alone with God as He spoke to my heart. And often I would hear my mother calling from inside "Zina, come in and eat!" I would sigh as I skipped over the hose on the lawn to stop the running water. I had no choice but to go inside. I suppose I was competing with Mr. Kahl and trying to make our lawn look as good as his. But no matter how green our grass was, it could never be like his.

My silent conversation with God was momentarily interrupted as I went inside, but He was never far from my thoughts.

And God didn't forsake me in the moments of my accident either. I remember lying there, unable to talk, see, or move, with chaos all around me. I was in shock, but God sustained me. In life, sometimes we go through situations that we can endure only by the grace of God. And only God has kept me. He stayed with me as I lay there on the street, my body broken, and in the hospital every night—going over what we would do, our plan for how to handle all of this.

I remembered what He told me as a child on my bike rides: *"I will never leave you nor forsake you,"* but that it would be hard. Otherwise, there is no way I could have endured such trauma and survive. Not at the tender age of sixteen. *Not without God.*

Welcome to My Nightmare

I woke up to my older brother Joe's face very early while still in the Pediatric Intensive Care Unit (PICU) and scribbled on a writing pad "Where am I?" I couldn't talk because I had a breathing tube down my throat. I had no idea where I was or how much time had passed. Covered in white sheets, I heard the sound of machines beeping and whirring.

"You're in a hospital bed," he told me. I read the sadness in his eyes.

Confused, I wrote "What happened?"

"You were in an accident."

"What kind of accident?" I didn't have any recollection of it, when it took place, or how long I was unconscious.

"You were hit by a car." His face told me it was the worst thing he ever had to say.

My hand scrawled out the unthinkable. "Why can't I move my legs?"

He purposefully did not respond.

At that moment, I knew my life would never be the same.

The breathing tube was painful, and I was almost always nauseous from it being stuck down my throat. It made me cough and gag and want to throw up, and oftentimes I did.

I had tubes in both nostrils that went down my throat and into my stomach—a nasogastric tube that was used as a feeding tube to administer drugs and a nasogastric aspiration tube that drained the stomach's contents of gastric secretions and swallowed air.

From the corner of one eye, I could see gunk moving out of my stomach and down the tube. From the corner of my other eye, I saw food agents going through the feeding tube and into my stomach. All the while, I still had the breathing tube, a feeding tube, a suction tube, and I was hooked up to various machines. My sister said they tied my hands together a few times in the beginning because I tried to pull the breathing tube out.

Rubber chest tubes were inserted through my sides to get rid of excess air in my lungs. As a result of surgery, air can fill up in the lungs, causing the lungs to collapse. I still have deep hole-like scars where the tubes were.

The most excruciating pain I've ever felt in my life was when the doctor pulled those tubes out, especially the left one. He pulled the right one out, then just a day or two later he pulled the left tube out while I was in the PICU. I cannot explain how painful it was when he pulled that left tube out. It only lasted a few moments, but the tear was so strong it felt like the doctor ripped my skin from me. I've never felt anything like it.

"Are you ready, Zina?" he said. "This is going to hurt but it'll be over in a second." He told me to take a deep breath in, followed by a strong exhale. As I exhaled he pulled the tube out. His empathy and compassion made all the difference. He was glad it was over and tried his best to comfort me.

One thing I've learned about being ill is that when you have the right care from people who are sensitive, it really helps. *Love is a force that is able to heal the worst of situations.* I wish for anyone sick or in the hospital to have the right care, the kind of care I was blessed to have at U of M.

As time went by my body started to heal. Although I couldn't completely feel my legs I still felt pain, especially in my knees where the scars were. The main side effect of spinal cord injury is paralysis. Even my voice was silenced due to the breathing tube. Looking back, I remember enduring this scary situation. I can still take my mind back to it and feel all those tubes and hear the sounds of beeping machines as I lay there, unable to move.

Guests filled my room often but I wasn't fully intact, especially the first few weeks—I was on a lot of morphine. I have no idea how else I would've endured such excruciating pain. There were staples in my knees and staples in my stomach that went around to my back like a curving railroad track; I had open scars where the fasciotomies were done.

People tell me "you're so strong" all the time. Perhaps I am; but for me to be here is a part of God's plan. He controls everything. We have to understand that everything happens by Him and for Him. I think sometimes people have this misconception that they are rewarded because of their efforts or hard work and things they do. Good things happen to them, and they get surprised when bad things occur. But God allows suffering sometimes. After all, no matter how much suffering I've been through, it's nothing compared to the suffering Jesus went through. We must acknowledge that any wealth, success, or achievements we have are given to us by Him.

It's so easy to get caught up in this "me" type thinking. The Bible says we are created in the image and likeness of Him. We can't ignore the reality of God. And we can't get angry when things don't go as planned. We all suffer—that is a part of life. Some more than others, yes, it's true. Some people seem to have it so good. Sometimes we wonder *why them and not me?* We have to trust in God's plan. He wants to bless us. He wants to be there for us and be our best friend. But we have to trust Him. I once heard a pastor say, "Even if we don't understand, in time He makes all things right."

Of course, this awareness didn't come all at once. I had a long journey ahead of me, but God would hold my hand every step of the way.

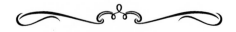

Chapter 2

Heaven on Earth—
in a Hospital

although I was admitted to the Pediatric Intensive Care Unit on October 18, 1994, I didn't get up to the Pediatric Medicine and Rehabilitation Unit until November 15. That was when they finally transferred me to a clear liquid diet and took me off the feeding tube. I was weaned off the ventilator on November 2. I couldn't eat solid food or drink more than ice chips in a Styrofoam cup in the PICU. My wounds and fractures were healing nicely, but I remained in my cervical collar because of the fracture to my vertebrae. I stayed at Mott Children's Hospital a little over three months.

They discharged me not long after my birthday on January 26, 1995. All the nurses came to me, expecting me to be happy. *Aren't you excited to go home?* their faces beamed. What they didn't know was that I was terrified inside. Deeply saddened, I cried alone at night. I've never liked to cry in front of others as I have always thought of it as a sign of weakness. It was just between God and me. Nighttime was when I prayed the most because it was quiet and I could focus more. It was in moments of silence that I felt the presence of the Lord the most. It was also when I heard from Him. The only distractions were when the nurses came in to flip me from one side in bed to the other to help prevent pressure sores, or to change the bandages/dressings on my stomach and legs.

Things were moving along well. I was healing up. It was peaceful at night. I didn't like the reason I was there, but I liked being in the silence and experiencing the peace. And I contemplated my future with Him.

What are we going to do, Lord? How will my life be? I had suffered this tragedy but I didn't know how to move forward and pick up the pieces. I needed Him to tell me. By now my friends were starting to visit less often; they still had their normal teenage lives. I feared I'd be a burden on my family.

Letters to God

Always faithful, God spoke to me alone each night and in the day through the love of others—the nurses, Mary Kay, my mom. He explained every step of the way, what we would do and how we would get through. I kept a journal, and each night at midnight— under my covers, with my flashlight in one hand and a pencil and pad in the other, with 10,000 Maniacs playing "These Are the Days" and "Garden of Eden" in the background—I would write.

> Dear God,
> I believe You are with me—listening to me and answering my prayers. I feel lucky. I have You here. That's because I've opened my heart, and I'm trying to more and more every day. I don't know how I got so lucky. Because before this accident I didn't know exactly how You worked. I was insecure because I didn't know who I was. But now it's like I have found myself, I know who I am, what I want, where I am going. And I'm sure of myself. I'm a different person. I know that I used to ask You to help me be a better person every night. And I believe my prayers were answered. I don't know. But no matter what, I'm thankful. How did I get so lucky for You to help me and save me from the accident? And help me see clearly? I know it came from You. There's a reason for this accident. I want to do something out of this world, like help sick people when I get older. I want to be a doctor. I believe I have a mission here.

Mott Children's Hospital became my home. I was safe there. Being in a wheelchair was okay. I accepted that my body was damaged. It took two or three nurses to turn me in bed from one side to the other, and a lift to put me in a wheelchair. *How are they going to send me home?* I wondered. When my discharge date drew near I felt upset, afraid. I wasn't walking yet! I wasn't back to the way I was before the accident. I thought they hadn't given me enough time. I had developed a system there. I had learned how to deal with spinal cord injury. Right when I began to get a handle on things, it was time to go home. I resented that.

I missed nearly my entire junior year due to the accident, but I really wanted to get my diploma with everyone else and graduate on time. So I attended all of my physical therapy sessions and learned how to cope. A schoolteacher would come to the hospital a few times a week and leave me with homework to make sure I completed my studies and got credits for my junior year.

My sister Kelly reached her ninth month of pregnancy—with her first child—during my hospital stay. On one of her regular visits, we were talking about baby names and I spontaneously suggested she name her daughter Faith. She loved the idea. She named her Fayth. *Faith is what brought me through.*

Yet just as I started to get comfortable at Mott, it was time to go home. My mind whirled with unanswered questions. *How will my life be in a wheelchair? What will become of me? How will I go back to school paralyzed? What will my friends think? Will I even have any?*

I was pretty. I was popular before this. *I have to go back to school in a wheelchair—for my senior year?* Everyone would be excited for prom and spring break. I was going to be disabled. Already the visits from my friends were lessening.

Life sometimes happens whether we are prepared or not. Life happened to me. I had one hope: my faith. And I held onto it. Until this day I still hold onto it. It's what has always brought me through. It's all I've ever known. It is huge. It's a gift from above. It's as if the hospital was a place to sort things out. My life had changed dramatically, and only God could help me.

Midway through my stay, I never wanted anyone to sleep at the hospital. My mother or sisters would spend weekends there in the beginning, but later I always asked them to leave. At sixteen, I was already independent and needed to be alone. I knew only God could get me out of this, and nighttime was my opportunity to pour out my heart to Him.

It wasn't until I got upstairs to 6 East, the Pediatric Medicine and Rehabilitation Unit, that I was trained to sit. Up till then I couldn't even sit on my own. They custom-made a thick, heavy back brace to hold me up and keep my spine in place. My spine not only broke at L1-L2, it shifted from the crash. The brace would help to straighten out my spine.

At the time, only two of my sisters were still at home, and one of my brothers would come and go. My parents had eight children including me, the youngest in the family. Half of my siblings were already out of the house, married, and had families of their own. Our home was not wheelchair-accessible. My parents did not know how to raise someone in a wheelchair.

Although I was born in the United States, my parents migrated here in 1970 from Baghdad, Iraq. Their nationality is Chaldean. Today, Christians in Iraq are a minority of about 5-7 percent, maybe even less.

My dad had a health scare or two before this when his doctor warned him it was vital for him to quit smoking and drinking. He quit smoking but he never quit drinking. My mother always took good care of him. Now she had to care for a sick child too. This was out of her realm. It was a season in my life where all I had was God. I knew that after the dust settled, the visits would lessen. Friends would carry on with their own lives. My care would add even more stress to everyone in my family.

While still in the PICU, I remember being shocked that my friends were going to school. *They're going to school without me?* I actually believed their lives had stopped because mine had come to a halt. I was out of touch with reality.

Now, however, I was no longer under that delusion. *What is to become of me?* I wondered. I knew I would watch everyone else pass me by. They would go to prom, spring break, and then onto college. I couldn't walk. Come on, when is it ever "cool" not to walk? *Who will want to hang out with me when I can't walk? Will I ever get married?* Life as I knew it had changed. I was now embarking upon a new life, and I knew things would never be the same.

I was certain of one thing though—I had God. I knew He heard me each and every time I talked to Him. I knew He would never let me go. I knew He would stay by my side. That was my security. Emotionally, I had to be steel—but not in my own strength.

The Truth at Last

As I prepared for my discharge, I often thought back over my time at Mott Children's and all that had happened to me in such a short period of time. During the first few weeks, in the PICU, day by day I grew closer to Regina, my primary nurse. My earliest memories were of her, waking up to find her taking care of my heavy, nearly lifeless body when I couldn't move— to adjust me, give me medications, change my dressings post-surgery. Despite my horrific condition, she just took control and kept being my nurse, strong yet also compassionate. I found solace in her strength.

She was the one who explained there were four stages of condition with critical being the worst, as I repeatedly asked her what was wrong with me. I remember her telling me when I reached a "stable" level. At sixteen, I never would have known what that meant had she not explained it to me.

God has sent people to help me at pivotal times by giving me the right word of encouragement or teaching or faith. Regina is one of those people. I call them my "angels on earth." I have been blessed with other angels who've helped me along the way. You will read about them in the following pages.

Regina was my anchor, and I clung to her for dear life. I didn't know what the next day would bring, if I would wake up, or how many more breaths I would take. I nicknamed her Regu for short, finding a way to joke in the midst of pain and unpredictability.

I kept asking why I couldn't move my legs; no one wanted to tell me. Some of the hospital staff urged my family to tell me for weeks, but no one wanted to. Finally one day Regina went into the waiting room and told my family that someone had to tell me why I couldn't move my legs.

At her bidding, my older sister Houda found the courage to tell me. Regina came in with her and they spoke words I will never forget.

"Look, Zina, I have to talk to you," Houda began, and Regina closed the door behind them. My sister looked nervous. "The doctors are saying you're never going to walk again," she confessed.

I started to cry. "Is that why I can't move my legs? Why can't I move my legs?" It was all I kept asking.

"Yeah, listen, they are saying you aren't going to walk," Houda continued, with Regina standing quietly behind her, hands clasped as if she were in prayer. Her presence was strong and gave my sister support. "But listen, you know about Jesus and you have faith. You can walk again."

I could hear my sister—I could see her mouth moving—but I couldn't fully comprehend what she was saying. *I would never walk?* As the words finally sank in it felt as if my whole world were crumbling, falling apart.

Regina stepped forward, her eyes shining. "Zina, listen, I had a dream and you were running to me in this dream. You kept saying, 'Regina, thank you, thank you, Regina, thank you!' And you were running to me in it." Regina was not only a nurse for many years in the PICU; she was also an ordained Baptist minister and woman of faith. My heart swelled as she continued. "The Lord Jesus can heal, and He gives me prophetic dreams about my patients sometimes." I trusted her and knew her words held true.

I felt as if these two strong women were carrying me out of this agony and terror that was so overbearing for a young girl. Through their love I was convinced. Houda later told me that when she first ran out after the accident to see me lying on the ground with blood gushing out, she thought *Oh my God, she's going to die!* And immediately she got a word from the Holy Spirit—before she even finished her thought—that declared *"NO SHE IS NOT. SHE IS GOING TO BE FINE."*

I can't explain how I felt in those moments. I could use the word *crushed* but even that would not be strong enough. It's a feeling I pray that no one ever has to experience. But my sister was right. I did know Jesus and I did have faith. I just had not realized how well I knew Him. Even on the days when I didn't feel He was near or wondered where He was—He was there all along. All those nights before my accident when I prayed to be a better person, I asked God to help me understand things because my surroundings had me confused. It all came down to this.

My sister and Regina did talk to me about Jesus and about having faith, but I don't know that anyone told me how to talk to God. I think it's just something I always knew from childhood. Because even though I didn't realize it, I was always talking to Him from a very young age. I always felt His presence and walked with Him.

I understood God's love and His healing capability. I saw it in everyone else. I felt it in the will He put in me to go forward despite this calamity. I was ready to take on the challenge and move forward with Him in faith. Devastated I had gone through this? Yes. But happy I had found my best friend. This is a poem I wrote to Him at that time:

GOD

GOD I am crying, crying out to you.
Will you help me, help me get through.
Through the hard times with faith, strength, and wisdom.
And be able to face whatever the outcome.
I will give my hardest to do what I think is best for me.
With everything I got, heart, mind, ability will you hold my hand

through this PLEASE?
But if in the end I will be upset, I'll be thankful, thankful for being
here with family and friends.
And thank you God we finally met.

Zina

Angels in White Coats

My stay in the hospital became a time of inner and outer healing, and God dropped "angels" in my path to help me along the way—my doctors.

For example, every time Dr. Geiger looked at me his face lit up. My family would start to tremble. *What is he going to say next? What is the news for today?* My future was bleak. But he was so nice I just wanted to talk with him. Every morning before the crack of dawn, Dr. Geiger and his team would come in while doing their rounds. I always woke up to the "angels in white coats" surrounding my bed.

"It's okay, Zina, go back to sleep," he would whisper. I just wanted to talk with him; he just wanted me to get my rest. He was so genuine it's no wonder he was a pediatric trauma surgeon. He had this keen ability to look danger in the face and defeat it with his smile. I remember looking at Dr. Geiger and thinking *You don't know what I'm going to do with all this, doc. This is not the end. You don't know what is to come of it. You don't know who I am.*

"Please, Dr. Geiger, let me have Raspberry Snapple Iced Tea today," I begged—the same as I did nearly every day. Maybe today was the day he would cave in, I secretly hoped.

He just looked at me, his eyes a mixture of compassion and firmness. "You know I can't let you do that, Zina…not yet." I knew the reason why: I was still on a feeding tube. Only allowed to have ice chips while in the PICU, my brother Joe would sneak Snapple to me in my ice cup. Eddie and Joe, my two eldest brothers, argued because Eddie wanted to follow the doctor's orders and not let me have any.

When the tubes came out I could finally have Snapple Iced Tea. Soon after, I got a letter in the mail from the Snapple spokeswoman with a T-shirt, a case of Raspberry Snapple Iced Tea, and a signed note. Dr. Geiger had written a letter to them. That was just his way.

Another "angel" in my sphere was Dr. Polley, one of the surgeons who operated on me during the twelve hours of emergency surgery right after my accident. I heard a lot about him from my family. He would hug my mom and dad every time he went to talk with them in the waiting room. Being of Greek descent, I think he felt compassion for my parents for not having the benefit of native English. He always went the extra mile and wanted to make sure they felt okay. My sisters said he would come in every day and check up on me in the beginning.

Dr. Farley, my pediatric orthopedic surgeon, worked on my spine during my emergency surgery. She fused my spine and inserted two rods and screws near the level of the break. My dad talked about how comfortable she made him feel when she came out of the operating room that day and said "I saved your daughter, Mr. Hermez." Right then he knew I would be all right, and that gave him relief.

Dr. Farley still follows up with me all these years later. I still go to Mott Children's Hospital for follow-up X-rays every four to five years. It's nice that she has stayed with me all these years, even though I'm now thirty-five years old. In 2012 she said the X-rays of my spine looked good, with no deterioration due to aging. She didn't even set a date for me to go back. She was so happy to see me, and a nurse practitioner who came in during my checkup remembered me. Whenever I'm there, they treat me as if I'm a celebrity.

My entire team of surgeons included: Dr. Arnold G. Coran, M.D., the surgeon-in-chief of C.S. Mott Children's Hospital at that time; Dr. Ronald B. Hirschl, M.D., now the Arnold G. Coran Professor of Surgery and head of the Section of Pediatric Surgery at the University of Michigan, as well as the surgeon-in-chief of Mott Children's Hospital (Dr. Coran still remains Professor Emeritus of Surgery); Dr. Theodore Z. Polley, M.D., a pediatric surgeon and clinical associate professor of surgery; Dr. Daniel H. Teitelbaum, M.D., a pediatric surgeon and professor of surgery; Dr. James D. Geiger, M.D., a pediatric surgeon and professor of surgery; Dr. Frances A. Farley, M.D., a pediatric orthopedic surgeon and professor of surgery; and Dr. Gregory P. Graziano, M.D., an orthopedic surgeon and associate professor of surgery on the adult unit.

All these doctors hold other titles, and most of them are affiliated with other hospitals as well. It amazes me that more than nineteen years later *all* of my surgeons are still there—walking the floors of Mott Children's, saving children, saving lives. I can't describe the gratitude I feel for them, whose hands helped save my life through Jesus. I am forever grateful.

I was on the phone one time while upstairs in the Pediatric Medicine and Rehabilitation Unit. As I talked, Dr. Polley came in to check up on me. I was going to end my phone call because

I was happy to see him, but he didn't want to interrupt me. He quickly examined my abdomen and made a quick exit, smiling and waving goodbye. It seemed I made his day by interacting like a normal teenager. Seeing him made mine.

The last time I saw him was after I was discharged from the hospital. Houda was driving me to U of M for X-rays with Dr. Farley, and we ran into Dr. Polley as we were walking in the doors. My sister didn't recognize him at first. I did right away.

"Zina!" he exclaimed. Amazed by how speedily I rolled down the ramp in my wheelchair, he said, "Look at you! I almost didn't even recognize you. You look so good and are going so fast."

My face lit up. I told him about my progress with therapy and how I was healing up. "And be sure to tell Dr. Geiger I said hello," I added.

"Have you been drinking any Snapple lately?" he asked with a wink, and we chuckled. This is what I wrote in my journal at the end of that day:

Tuesday, May 16, 1995, 11:45 p.m.
I guess I've come to realize that pain is just a part of my life nowadays. Yet most of the time physical pain is easier to handle than mental pain. I have a mixture of both right now. I had my X-rays done today. Dr. Farley said everything looks great and for me to go back in six months and see how my rods are doing, if they bother me or not. She said they might take one out…

I saw one of the pediatric surgeons that was with Dr. Geiger's team today, Dr. Polley. I said hi to him and he said he barely recognized me because I looked so good. He asked me how therapy was. He asked me if my stomach had healed up. He was concerned. I told him to say hi to Dr. Geiger. And he asked me if I've been drinking Snapple lately. We laughed as he walked and I wheeled away. I was about to cry. Whenever I see the doctors, any one of them who saved my life, I want to cry. It's really touching for me. I have this love for them. They are wonderful people— Mott is the closest public place to heaven. The people there are wonderful.

We also visited Mott Children's upstairs at the PM &R Unit, and Julie, Annette, Robin, and all of my nurses were up there. Everyone told me how good I looked, and I wasn't even having one of my better days. I had a lot of pain in my legs today. It is wonderful I can feel them, but at the same time it can get nerve-wracking. That was my day; a lot happened in one day. I also have a lot of pressure on me about going back to school. I have to achieve. Two big inspirations in my life are Dr. Polley and Dr. Geiger...

I remember how safe I used to feel at Mott Children's. I loved being there, not for the reasons I was there but for the love and support. I never experienced that kind of love before. As awkward as it seems I was happy. Not happy with my situation, not happy with what happened to me—having broken legs, a broken spine, paralysis, and all this injury—but happy with the love that surrounded me. The love on that unit was incomparable. It emanated from the doctors, the nurses, even the families of children who were ill. There was this energy I can't explain, but it translated into a lot of love. It's no wonder my doctors are still walking those floors.

Another journal entry I wrote before I was discharged from the hospital:

January 22, 1995

Today is Sunday. It is 12:30 a.m. and I'm sitting here in my hospital bed with a flashlight in the dark, listening to 10,000 Maniacs and Counting Crows, writing, the same routine...

I love the outcome of this. I've learned how great God and people, or God's people, are. The type of people I associate with. I feel so full of love. He's putting this love for everyone in my heart.

My left leg is getting pretty strong. I can hold it up in the air for a few seconds at a time. My right one is coming along, it's just moving slower. It always has. I thank God it's moving. I should be getting out around early February. Gretchen, my physical therapist, said they will put me on braces around February or March.

In time, I know I'll walk again. I have God on my side. I've really been touched by God. It's the best feeling. I realize how precious life is. I appreciate everything and everyone now. I feel like a different person. I think in everybody's life there's a point where they really find God. And I'm lucky I did at such an early age. I'll never take life for granted and try to enjoy every minute of it.

The truth is I never wanted to leave Mott's. Robin and Julie, my nurses, would look at me with huge smiles and say, "Aren't you happy you're going home soon?" I always smiled back but I wanted to cry inside. I was scared. I was handicapped, and I knew it would be hard for my family to take care of me. I didn't know how to interact with friends now that I was in a wheelchair.

I knew that walking was possible but it was not going to happen overnight. I wanted to stay at the hospital until I got better. I wanted to stay there until I walked again, even if it took the rest of my life! I felt that them keeping me there just over three months was not fair. Then they decided to send me home early. I didn't feel well enough to go home. I wanted to stay there with my doctors and nurses and God by my side. I didn't want to enter the real world. I wanted to stay in the hospital, protected, where others understood me. I wanted to do therapy in the day and write at night. But unfortunately I had to go home.

I had a tough road ahead of me, but I knew that with God by my side—and with my journals, praying, reading the Bible, and my faith—I would be okay. No matter how scared I was or how much pain I had in my legs, I knew I would make it through. God promised me I would, and God always keeps His promises. He cannot tell a lie. And from the beginning Jesus told me in my heart I would walk. No matter how many friends left, no matter who turned their back on me or didn't want to hang out anymore, I knew I had one job to do: to press on.

A Twitch in My Leg and a Divine Soul Visit

They were all there—sisters, my mom, nurses—and I still couldn't move. The same feeling I'd had for weeks, no movement, heaviness in my body and legs, paralysis. The pain in my knees from staples that held my skin together after surgery kept me up at night, oftentimes with screams. Gauze covered the open wounds in my lower legs where the fasciotomies were performed.

Every hour the nurses rolled me over in bed to keep my blood flowing and to prevent pressure wounds. In the beginning it took two nurses to roll me over and sometimes a sister too. The bandages had to be changed a few times each day. When I could finally shower I only had a light bath, and a machine literally carried me into the tub. I could not move. Every time I moved from my bed to the wheelchair I needed a harness.

As time went by I moved up to the Pediatric Medicine and Rehabilitation Unit (PMRU). I kept getting better, and everyone was impressed by my progress. In physical therapy they were teaching me how to sit up and how to do bed-to-wheelchair transfers. I remember them timing how long I could sit. At first it was barely for a minute; we were counting the seconds. I had been in bed for so long. Plus I had all those injuries and paralysis. At times I thought, *If I can't even sit, how will I walk?* Yet my faith was strong. I didn't know how but I knew some way I would get there.

Every movement in the beginning, especially those first few weeks—even an inch, a centimeter—sent excruciating pain through my knees because of the staples. No matter what, I did not want them bent. I was so horrified by the pain I constantly had a fear of anyone touching my knees. If they did I would scream. My sister and one of the nurses kept telling me how good it was that I felt them because they weren't completely numb.

And in the midst of all that suffering, one day it happened. My miracle came. With everyone in the room, my left leg twitched. It was hard to see at first; you could barely discern it. But as I kept practicing moving my leg I showed everyone. "Look, look, my leg moved!" I was stubborn and had been fighting them to move for weeks. This became routine for me, even though some of the staff told my family to tell me I would not walk again.

But with no feeling, and supposedly dead muscularly, my left leg twitched. And the more I did it the more noticeable it became. My left leg came back alive! Everyone reacted. My sisters cried, some people clapped, my nurses were happy. This was a miracle that astonished everyone, including me, and it flooded me with peace. I knew somehow things would be all right.

Miracle No. 2

My second big miracle came from Dennis, a man who worked with me at the Strawberry Hills Fruit Market in Farmington Hills, Michigan, before my accident. It was my first job. I worked there part-time after school as a cashier and stocker. Dennis was African-American and in his early to mid-forties. There was something about him I couldn't quite put my finger on, yet I knew he was different in a special way.

Dennis had an inner peace about him. At sixteen, I couldn't understand. He always had a smile on his face and was always singing hymns to God. I thought this was strange. I never knew anyone that way. I couldn't understand why he was always so happy.

Each time he saw me in the aisle he made me smile. "Zina, smile, let me see that beautiful smile! Come on, smile!" he would say. I couldn't walk past him unless I smiled. After my accident, he brought flowers and came to visit me on the weekends, even though I hadn't known him for very long. He also brought prayer booklets and talked to me about God and faith.

My left arm was stuck at a 90-degree angle from the crash. The orthopedic therapists could not get it straight. They tried for weeks. One day Dennis got up and stood next to my bed. He held my arm gently but firmly and began to pray intently. He started speaking in what Christians call "tongues." Though I'd never heard anyone use tongues before, I was not afraid. I trusted him. I didn't understand all that was happening, but I knew he was a good man.

My arm started to get warm as he slowly stretched it. I felt more and more heat as he straightened it with both hands. Dennis was praying and talking to God all the while, and after fifteen minutes or so my arm became totally straight. If God didn't heal my arm through Dennis that day, I never would've gotten up on parallel bars. I never would've been able to use crutches as I do now. Imagine trying to get up on bars or walk with walking devices with an arm stuck at 90 degrees? It's not possible. Dennis, through the power of prayer, performed a healing work on me. *I thank God for the angels He's sent along the way.*

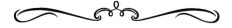

Chapter 3

Life after the Accident: Facing the Great Unknown

April 29, 1995

Living…

You live your lives the way you choose…

I sit here with not much left to lose.

You live your lives and enjoy every day,

I don't know exactly what I did to deserve being this way…

You'll have your fun and live your teenage lives in every way,

While I sit here day by day, all I do is pray.

g oing back to school was hard. I had missed nearly my entire junior year. But being homeschooled for a portion of my time at Mott Children's helped me get some credits for my junior year.

In the summer of 1995, I felt the pressure mounting because of the new school year—my senior year—that was fast approaching. I really wanted to graduate on time with everyone else in my class. When I got out of the hospital, I stayed home and did physical therapy and tried my best to adjust to my new life in a wheelchair. I really did not want to go back to school. Not the way I was—handicapped.

I wanted to be with my friends; some of them I had been in school with since junior high or even elementary. Of course, everyone knew about what happened to me, and I felt bad. My story made the local news, and columns were written about me in the newspaper. *The Popular, Active Student Who Got Hit by a Car!* I felt I let everyone down: the school, my teachers, the council, my friends. *How could I get hurt?*

"There are some things that just happen, beyond reasoning, beyond intellect, beyond resolution. Things like calamities, destructions, hurricanes, and disasters," says Bishop T.D. Jakes in his sermon "Beyond the Blame."

"The Bible says rain will fall on the just and unjust. Some stuff just happens to you. Stop trying to rationalize everything."

I held onto those words.

Accidents happen. We can't reverse them. If I could I would. It's hard to always feel that way though. I've held onto guilt. As time has gone by, I've learned to make peace. I can't explain how. It's taken God's grace to release me. I remind myself that grace tells me everything will be all right. I'm forgiven. I'm free.

Our home on Gramercy Court was not handicap-accessible so I had to live in an apartment with my sisters Houda and Sandy for two years until our new home was built. Sandy, the second youngest, is seven years older than me. Houda is fifteen years older than me. I was sad I could no longer live in our house on Gramercy Court. My parents had been planning to build a new house anyway, and my accident gave them a reason to move. I tried to think of it as a new beginning, but I still felt depressed.

Before our new home was built, my parents temporarily stayed in one apartment while my sisters and I stayed in another. There were too many of us to share one apartment. Our new home was also in a nice neighborhood and within fifteen minutes driving distance from our old home on Gramercy Court.

Throughout the first few years after the accident, the doctors were impressed by my speed of recovery. At the apartment with my sisters, I would take my walker outside and wear my braces and take short walks. At first I couldn't do too many steps, just a few, and I needed someone outside with me. But as time went by I practiced more and increased the number of steps. My goal was to graduate high school on time with my class and walk across the stage with a walker to receive my high school diploma.

My parents found a property to build on, and the idea was to make sure the new house was handicap-accessible. It was not. I really did not want it that way. You had to walk up stairs to get into the house, and there was a walk-out basement. The deck in the back had stairs leading down to a patio. I wanted to walk as best I could and didn't mind doing the stairs. I saw it as strengthening exercise and another way to heal. I also spent most of my time on the main floor because that's where my bedroom was in the new house. I liked to hang out in there, talk on the phone, watch TV, and write in my journals.

By the time we moved into our new home, when I was nineteen, I could hold onto two railings and walk up stairs! I wore leg braces up to my knees while doing them, but early on I was blessed to be able to walk.

Behind the Wheel Again

Although I was driving at sixteen at the time of my accident, I didn't have a car. I would ask to borrow one from my family, but it was rare that I got to. My dad sometimes gave me his old light-blue late 1970s Lincoln. It was nothing fancy, and I would have to pull it off to the side of the road to add coolant often because it would overheat while I was driving and stop on me.

My friends would laugh, surprised that I knew how to do that, but I had no choice. It was the only car I had when I was able to borrow one. Each time I was able to fix the car and get us home. My mother often commissioned my brother-in-law, David, to pick me up from work or take me to friends' houses. He picked me up and dropped me off when it was requested of him. He was nice about it too.

But I could no longer use my legs to drive after the accident. It wasn't until I was about nineteen that I started driving again—this time by learning how to drive with a hand-control.

My case manager at that time, Linda, suggested I learn this new skill. The driving instructor would pick me up at our new house and take me out to practice driving. Until then, Houda and my mom always had to take me to doctors' appointments and physical therapy sessions. Learning how to drive really helped me. Later, when I started taking courses at the local community college, I could put my wheelchair in and out of my car and drive myself back and forth to school. It was nice.

It upset me that I could no longer live in my home on Gramercy Court. That was where I grew up. That was where I played football with the neighborhood kids down the street after school. That was where my role model, Pat Rogers, would spend time with us kids to teach us how to throw a football, or simply hang out with us in the green room playing Monopoly. That was where my childhood best friend, Melissa Dean, and I played tennis or board games. That was where I rode my bike up and down the street, talking silently to God and learning to hear His voice. My home on Gramercy Court meant a lot to me, and I had to leave. It made me very sad.

Going back to school my senior year in a wheelchair was one of the hardest things I've ever had to do in my life. It took a lot of courage, but I found it. My friend Marzel was also on the Multicultural/Multiracial Community Council at school my junior year. We were both in the same grade and very excited to serve. I was only able to serve for around a month that year. His being on the panel made it more fun. He and his dad would drop me off at home after our council meetings. That was so nice and I remember what a great help it was for me. Marzel was kind and his dad was too. We were able to laugh together and act as plain teens do. We really got along.

I was honored that Mr. Peolke chose me, and I thought perhaps it was because I had helped the kids with English as a second language in middle school. Looking back, he may have picked up on my energy and how badly I wanted to do well that year. I was not far from graduation. I wanted to go on to college and get into a good school. I didn't know exactly what I wanted to do, but I thought that teaching would be nice. I knew I wanted to have a career.

My mother was a stay-at-home mom and didn't have the benefit of native English. She could not read and write in English. She knew the basics like the alphabet and she could sign her name. Her life was spent at home cooking and cleaning and raising us kids. I remember how we got lost one time on our way home from a relative's house. My mother couldn't read the expressway signs. She would go from place to place by memorization. Since those places were familiar to her, she knew where she was.

But this one time there were additions to the expressway that she did not know about. It took us over an hour to get home and it was late at night. I was only in grade school but I was reading the signs to her—she still didn't know where we were. We pulled over to ask someone and finally made our way home. It was hard for her to communicate in English back then. We felt vulnerable, and I could tell my mom was really nervous too.

I think that experience always stayed in the back of my mind. I decided I never wanted to feel that powerless again. I promised myself to do my best in school and learn as much as I could.

I was not able to attend the assembly with all the students, teachers, principals, and representatives. My friends said that on the day of the big event, the council stood and recognized my absence, sharing a few words about me. All the students in the gymnasium stood and applauded. Mr. Peolke spoke about how motivated I was to bring us all together. He said he was always impressed at my comments during the preparation meetings.

Back to School—in a Wheelchair

I didn't want to go back to school in a wheelchair but I had to. I knew my inner circle of friends would not accept me. I feared that they would think they were too good, or that I would be a burden to them. I was right. I knew things would change and they did.

Life is hard enough. Not being able to walk. Not being able to move. It's one of the worst things that could happen to you. Paralysis is eye-opening, a nightmare to say the least. Some nights I would wake up out of my sleep and think it was all a dream— only to find it was real when I saw my wheelchair planted next to me.

I wasn't sure how everyone would react to my wheelchair, especially in the beginning. I looked different now. I didn't feel pretty. I always loved fashionable clothes and cool shoes. Now I was sitting in a wheelchair and it really affected my self-esteem. I was scared the students would laugh at me.

To my surprise though, my first day was totally opposite. Kristen, one of the girls I knew from elementary school, was so happy to see me. As soon as she saw me in the hallway she smiled brightly and gasped "Zinaaa!" She ran up to me and hugged me tight. It was so nice, especially since I no longer had my group of best girlfriends. Kristen was naturally popular, and the other kids were happy to see me too. They all surrounded me in a huge circle, full of excitement and friendly banter. I knew right then I would make it through the school year.

These were some of the same kids who after my accident responded with cards, flowers, posters, and phone calls. I felt like those students really stood by me. My cards and letters are still saved in my closet. They are treasures.

When I returned, many of the students welcomed me warmly, and that felt so good. I still had friends. I still had people who cared about me. By that time, the circle of friends that I hung out with from middle school had already abandoned me. They came around and visited in the hospital and stayed in contact for a couple of months. But our friendships had already diminished by the time I got back to school.

I wasn't able to attend a full day of school when I returned. I would leave after lunch to do a few hours of physical therapy. My generous teachers and principals really wanted me to get better and succeed, so they allowed me to leave early as part of my recovery. They were all rooting for me.

With all the anxiety I had about returning to school, the welcome back with open arms felt nice. I think that could've had something to do with why my group of best friends left. Especially when I got back to school, it was very obvious. They didn't like the attention I was getting from the students, teachers, and principals. Subtly, but not unrecognizably, they just did not come around me—even to say hello in the hall. I had been cast out, voted off.

Whenever they saw me, they would look over my head or pretend I wasn't there or just walk away. I even caught them rolling their eyes sometimes. They had already stopped calling long before then. They were too busy at parties and too busy hanging out with each other and doing normal teenage things. And I always felt they had some irritation toward me because of so many others praising my strength.

Graduation day arrived and I woke up with butterflies in my stomach. I was ready—I was going to achieve my goal of walking across the platform to receive my diploma.

"Zina, hurry, it's time to go!" Houda called from down the hall as I made final preparations, making sure my hair and makeup looked just right.

When I graduated later that evening, I did walk with a walker to receive my diploma. I wore leg braces up to my knees, but I accomplished my goal! All the teachers and of course Mr. Peolke were there. I was nervous as my older brother Joe wheeled me up to the wheelchair lift. They put my walker on the stage so I could stand up from my wheelchair and walk. A lot of eyes were on me; there must have been a few hundred people in that auditorium. The cavernous room grew silent—so quiet you could hear a pin drop.

I got up to the stage on a lift, grabbed the walker from my wheelchair, and slowly stood to my feet. With a significant limp, I walked up to Mr. Peolke to receive my high school diploma. I remember him crying noticeably. I hoped it wasn't because he was sad for me. I wanted him to be happy. As Mr. Peolke handed me the diploma, the auditorium erupted in cheers and thunderous applause. Everyone stood to their feet. Houda and Sandy cried. My mom and dad were proud of me. They knew this was the day, the milestone, that meant so much to me.

Grief Turned to Joy

I had lost a lot physically, and losing my best friends affected me badly. I didn't understand why they didn't want to hang out with me anymore. It had felt so good those first few months when they came to visit or even gave a simple phone call. Life truly is about the friends who *stay* and the love they provide us.

As I reflect upon those years, all the suffering I went through at that young age was definitely hard. But I would not want to give back the closeness I felt with the Lord. I'm not happy about all that happened to me. I wish I didn't have any physical limitations at all. I would've gone out on more outings. I would've spent less time exercising and enjoyed more time with friends. But if it hadn't happened, I'm not sure I would've spent as much time with God.

When we are sick, we feel close to Him. We still love Him in our heart even when we are not, but we may be too wrapped up and busy in our own lives to spend time with Him. Even in my busy life now, I sometimes struggle with finding just fifteen minutes a day for devotional prayer. We all need God. When we feel well we may not realize *how much* we actually need Him. It's a part of human nature.

As a teen, those years were vital for me—to read and study Scripture, to listen to live prayer through the radio most nights, and to talk to God daily. I would not have come this far without doing those things. I've carried them into my adulthood. It has gotten me through. I have rejoiced with God in the good and the bad. When we are able to do that, when we have the gift of being able to be happy and sad with God, it is immeasurable.

In every race there is a finish line. An athlete who wants to win a championship has to train for endless hours. It can cause a lot of pain, but there is sweet victory at the end. I have tasted it. Some may wonder how. The Bible teaches that the greater the sorrow, the greater the joy. Why? Because joy and suffering are interchangeable, that's why. *"Most assuredly, I say to you that you will weep and lament, but the world will rejoice; and you will be sorrowful, but your sorrow will be turned into joy" (John 16:20).*

My First Holy Communion at eleven years old.

*At my home on Gramercy Court, trying to force
a smile. How could I have known that in less
than a year my life would be forever changed?*

Celebrating my sixteenth birthday party at my best friend's house.

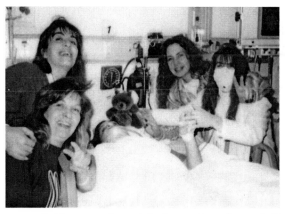

Surrounded by sister love: (clockwise from lower left) Sue, Houda, Sandy, and Kelly. Still early on after the accident.

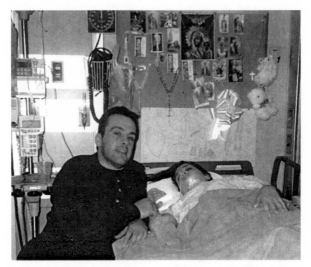

*With my brother, Ed. Doing much better at the Pediatric
Medicine and Rehabilitation Unit 6 East.*

*A surprise visit from two
University of Michigan college athletes.*

My seventeenth birthday party at C.S. Mott Children's Hospital. Trying to stay positive for the kids.

Regina, my unforgettable nurse.

Senior picture after high school graduation. Feeling successful!

*I was so honored. Risa, my friend from college,
still asked me to walk in her wedding.*

*I made it! Graduated college with
my bachelor's degree at Oakland
University, 2004 (pictured with
administration staff).*

Father Robert C. Dressman, S.J.,
whose words have never left me.

Me today.

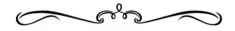

Chapter 4

Physical Therapy—My Progression and Recovery

June 7, 1995

What's important is self-image. Not whether I am walking or not. I mean…walking is a very admirable and practical goal that I can achieve; however, self-image is what we project of ourselves which comes from within. If we can't love ourselves on the inside, it doesn't matter whether we are standing, sitting in a wheelchair, running, crawling, or walking. Our self-image will be poor and not positive, but negative…

O ver the course of the last nineteen years, I have attended four or five major facilities for physical therapy. I never gave up on my goal of walking as best I could; nor did I give up hope for my recovery. I've always believed "persistence is the key to success." The phrase couldn't be truer, especially when you're dealing with a spinal cord injury.

After I was discharged from Mott Children's Hospital, I continued there with outpatient physical therapy for several weeks. Since it was in Ann Arbor, Michigan, and I lived a good forty-five minutes away, the commute back and forth was hard on my sister Houda. My case manager, Linda, found another place for us to attend that was closer by.

When I started attending the new facility, Barnum Rehabilitation Center in Birmingham, Michigan, I was seventeen years old and it was 1995. Houda didn't mind the drive as much because it was less than twenty minutes from our apartment.

At Barnum I did intense water and land therapy, attending five days a week during my senior year after a half-day at school. After a couple hours of physical therapy, I would come home exhausted, have something to eat, take a nap, wake up, and do my homework. Then I would repeat the process all over again the next day.

I started pool therapy with my recreational therapist, Karen. The first time I got in the water my legs were so buoyant, especially my right. As soon as it hit the water it just bounced right back up.

It took some time for me to be able to bear weight on that right leg and walk on it in the water. In the water, you carry much less body weight. My core would come forward because of the weakness in my abs and back, so I would hold onto Karen's shoulders and she would hold onto my hips and walk backwards while facing me. Karen would have to step on my foot with her knee digging into mine to hold it back from collapsing in order for me to take a step onto that right foot.

Learning to Walk

It was at Barnum that I learned to walk short hallway distances with a walker. The therapy got me mobile enough that after I learned how to drive with hand-controls, I was able to at least take my walker out and drive to a friend's house or to a restaurant—somewhere not requiring too much walking—to meet a friend. It was nice not having to take a wheelchair with me. That felt very freeing. It took a couple of years after my accident to gain this kind of independence. I also began taking classes at the local community college. My life was beginning to feel somewhat normal again.

Although my leg braces were still high, I loved having the ability to walk. They were heavy and thick and came up to my knees with straps, and the ankles were bulky, fixed, and unable to move. Still, they were better than the original braces I wore at Mott Children's when I was inpatient there. Those braces were called KAFOs, and they were *seriously* high.

KAFOs are full-length braces that reach up to your pelvis and help you lift your hip to clear your foot and take a step. These devices are used on patients requiring more stability of the hip and lower torso, due to paralysis. Often they are used by adults and children with spinal cord injury or cerebral palsy. Once I adjusted my weight from one side to the other, the braces were designed to lift the opposite leg. They provide maximum assistance for people with spinal cord injury when trying to walk.

Bulky and not meant to be taken out in the community, KAFOs are mainly used in physical therapy. They are stiff because the knee can be kept locked so as not to bend, but some KAFOs do have an option to bend at the knee. They are uncomfortable because of all the support. You can only walk with them for so long. I had my KAFOs cut down to knee level while attending Barnum because I had improved!

As I strengthened year after year, my braces got cut down and changed several times. Each time they have gotten shorter because I persisted in requesting the least amount of assistance to walk. I would have custom-made orthopedic braces. One doctor said that when nerves are regenerating, every year they grow back about an inch. That could explain why year after year I gained strength and endurance, and so I cut the braces often and walked with less support.

It seemed that people I saw in physical therapy often walked with full-length support they may not have needed. I felt that if they just asked for a reevaluation, they may have had shorter braces too, thus strengthening their legs. Whether or not a patient wants to cut down their braces is not a common question for physical therapists to ask. It's a question the patient needs to be proactive about.

With all my progress, it's still not easy for me to stand up with no assistance. The interesting thing is that I can walk on crutches, and now I am learning how to walk with one cane. If you take away my walking devices—unless I'm holding onto something—it is hard to just stand there for a long period of time. One of my therapists said, "How can you walk when it is hard for you to stand?"

I said, "I know, right?" We laughed. She was surprised that I could walk with one cane but had trouble standing. If I have a cane or crutches, I can stand for a long time. It is harder to stand with no support. With training and practice though, I can stand a little bit longer.

Today I wear AFOs, which are an ankle-foot orthosis. They mainly provide ankle support. Small, low-profile, and lightweight, they have a spring. The ankle does not completely bend but it allows you to flex at the joint so your foot can move and you get ankle-to-toe action. These are the least amount of brace support I have ever worn. I've had them for a couple of years now. In 2013 my physical therapist purchased Figure 8 braces for me. They are made of elastic and worn by people with minor sports injuries—the most low-profile brace I have ever practiced walking with.

Barnum is where I learned how to swim again too. Swimming has a lot of health benefits. It can help you tone and lose weight, and it doesn't put stress on your joints, according to the Centers for Disease Control. Barnum helped me learn how to swim, walk in the water, and get to where I could take out my walker and do some distance.

College-bound and Beyond

After I graduated high school I took the summer off. Then I started taking classes at the nearby community college in the fall. Driving at the time, I took my wheelchair to college because the distance from the parking lot to my classes was still pretty far for me to walk with a walker. But all the physical improvement helped me continue with my goal of achieving in school, and I was able to graduate with my associate's degree in general studies.

In 2001 I moved away to college; I was twenty-three years old. My sister Sandy lived with me and we shared a two-bedroom apartment in Auburn Hills, Michigan, that was really close to campus—literally across the street. Houda had gotten married by that time, and it was convenient for Sandy to live with me. She had never lived on her own either, and she wanted to experience that too. My parents worried about us and didn't want us to go away. But I wanted to fulfill my dream of having a career, a deep-seated desire ever since high school.

I had already completed my associate's degree; now I wanted to further my studies, and Oakland University (OU) was a great school. It was not too far from our parents' home, and Sandy and I could still see Mom and Dad on the weekends and visit with family.

By living near campus, it would be easier to drive back and forth to class, go home for lunch sometimes, complete the paperwork for financial aid, make new friends, and get the full college experience. Since I was putting my wheelchair in and out of the car up to five or six times a day in between classes, it just seemed like the best thing for me to do. It worked out really well, and being so close to the campus was very convenient for me.

OU had a new recreational center on campus with top-of-the-line weight and exercise machines for cardio and strengthening, and I went there to maintain my physical therapy with a trainer. I also used the workout facilities in my apartment complex.

My trainer, Todd, and I would take long walks around campus with my walker, reaching several hundred feet with a few sitting breaks in between. It was great exercise though because the campus was very big. To be able to walk around that campus was a great accomplishment. I did one-hour core exercises during my training sessions, some machines, and then my trainer and I would walk outside. We would talk about our hopes and dreams. He wanted to continue to help others through medicine. I wanted to write a book about my life's journey.

The best part was that Todd had a lot of faith and he enjoyed working with me. He appreciated the benefits of helping people injured badly. He began working on his doctorate in physical therapy and became a physical therapist. I felt honored that working with me helped him make that career decision, and now his positivity and impact have spread.

I attended Oakland University from ages twenty-three to twenty-six, and in 2004 I received my Bachelor of Arts degree in English with a history minor. I used my degree to teach.

I loved going to school there. I made new friends. The classes were interesting. It was a new beginning. I had lost my best friends in high school, and I wanted to start over again. Redefine my life. I loved my English classes; I got to read literature, oftentimes historical literature, and a lot of it was about different writers or people who have made an impact. I got to learn more about Christianity, and the extensive reading broadened my knowledge of it.

In addition, with a minor in history the classes would sometimes overlap and I would get to learn the same thing twice. Something I was reading in a literature class would show up on the history syllabus. I really liked that. I got to learn about American classic writers such as Henry David Thoreau, Edgar

Allan Poe, Ralph Waldo Emerson, Frederick Douglass, Sylvia Plath, and others.

When I graduated college, I moved back home with my parents for two years and attended a few other places for physical therapy. At twenty-eight I moved out again and got my own apartment fifteen minutes away from my mom and dad, so I saw them often. One of the places I attended while living at my parents' was called The Recovery Project. I went there for about six months, but I have always maintained a fitness membership.

In my apartment complex now, we have a nice clubhouse with weights, walking machines, and an indoor and outdoor pool. I have access to all the exercise equipment I need. By living here, I still have the ability to exercise, even if I am not going to physical therapy every day. Doctors typically do not write scripts for five days a week of physical therapy. I had to be active on my own in exercise. When you have a spinal cord injury, it is crucial to exercise.

Over the years I increased my minutes on the treadmill. I'm up to forty minutes of cardio: twenty on the treadmill and twenty on the elliptical back to back. My goal is to reach an hour of straight walking on the treadmill or elliptical machine. It does take quite a bit of energy from me, and if I miss the gym for even a week or two I notice the difference in my body. The longer I go without workouts, the more it affects me.

Another improvement has been holding onto the treadmill with only one hand while using the machine. The year 2012 was the first time I could do that. Granted, I am only letting go for about a minute at a time, lifting my right hand up and then putting it back down. I am still not able to lift my left hand yet. I believe I will be able to do that soon.

This means I am gaining strength in my gait, back, and trunk. It happened right around Christmastime. I felt like it was God's present to me. The more I can walk on a moving treadmill with one hand and build up my energy, the easier it will be to walk with a cane and then hopefully walk one day with no walking device.

One of the last major facilities I attended is The Rehabilitation Institute of Michigan (RIM), which is part of the Detroit Medical Center (DMC). DMC consists of several hospitals, and RIM is one of them. The institute's Center for Spinal Cord Injury Recovery (CSCIR) helps people reach "maximum recovery." I did really well there, starting in late 2008 and finishing in mid-2010.

Many people in wheelchairs would ask how I got to the point of being upright and walking so much, even with a walker or crutches. First I attributed it to my faith in God, and I would tell the patients how far He brought me. Then I would describe the different levels of therapy I had to go through and how hard I had to work. Some marveled. I often got positive feedback. The patients I talked to wanted to get insight because their goal was also to stay on their feet as much as they could.

CSCIR is unique in that it is a three-hour intensive-recovery program. You are working out for three hours straight. They set you up with a physical therapist and trainer, but you spend most of your time with your trainer, and if (s)he needs help, there may be additional trainers to help you. Some people come from other states to do the program. It is said to be one of the best intensive-recovery programs in the nation.

There were a lot of young people there, and some were around my age. Unfortunately, the common age for spinal cord injury is young. According to Mikeutley.org, "Spinal-cord injury primarily affects young adults. Most injuries occur between the ages of 16 and 30; the average age at injury was 28.7 years. However, as the median age of the general population of the United States has increased the average age has also steadily increased over time. Since 2005, the average age at injury is 41 years."

Never Settle for Status Quo!

At CSCIR, everyone was fighting to walk, fighting to move. Watching them inspired me. We all shared one common goal—to achieve healing there. I really got to see these people for who they were, not only their wheelchairs.

The reason I mostly see the wheelchair when I look at people's physical challenges is because I can't stop seeing mine. It's my un-acceptance of a wheelchair that has brought me so far. At the same time, I wish I accepted it more. I want to start seeing it the way everyone else does, as okay. I guess not accepting it has been my motivation to walk, but I have also struggled with accepting myself because of it. I know my wheelchair is not a part of me. It's not a part of my makeup or who I am. Oftentimes I worry that others can't see past it. I think it's me who can't.

I saw some of the patients with their camouflage KAFO braces and younger girls with their pink wheelchairs. I have always kept wheelchairs and crutches at the most unnoticeable color I could, usually black, white, or neutral. I never wanted to bring more attention to my imperfection. The acceptance level of some of these patients even helped me to think of my injury as not being so bad. They were simply people caught in a bad situation who wanted to get well.

Just as I have always worn the most minimal brace support possible, I have also never taken any medication for depression or anxiety. I've never liked to take medication, period. I've only taken it temporarily when a doctor suggested it and it was apparent I needed medication to get well. I am never on any drug unless it's an antibiotic for an occasional infection or something like that.

God has always been my form of therapy. The Holy Bible says, *"But seek first the kingdom of God and His righteousness, and all these things shall be added to you. Therefore, do not worry about tomorrow, for tomorrow will worry about its own things. Sufficient for the day is its own troubles"* (Matthew 6:33-34).

I think it's best for all of us to try to live by that. When I have rare moments where I need to go in my room and cry I do, and within minutes I start to feel better because I pray. I talk to God. I read the Bible. I call a friend. I exercise. I study. I do whatever I have to do.

At CSCIR, my ultimate goal was to walk as best I could. Recovery is a process. In order to walk with nothing, I must first get functional with one cane.

When I started at the CSCIR in late 2008, I was taking steps with one cane, but the minute they saw me walking even only ten steps with it at my evaluation appointment, they made me stop. They said I was not ready because my posture was bad. I have always had some lordosis, or curvature of the spine in the lumbar region. It's a result of the accident, surgery, and sitting in a wheelchair.

It's kind of difficult to walk with one cane when you have this structural problem, as you feel your body throwing you forward a little. If you don't have strong abs and a strong back, how do you hold yourself up? This needed to be corrected. That was one of my major problems. Fortunately, in the time I spent there it improved significantly.

Other problems were the shift in my pelvis and scoliosis in my spine. I also had a leg length discrepancy. In the beginning of physical therapy at Barnum, I was told I had a six-inch leg length difference in measurement. If I sat with my legs stretched out in front of me on the table, my left leg was shorter than the right.

After a lot of deep-scar-tissue massage by a therapist at CSCIR, we were able to correct some of the problems. The massage tore down the layers of scar tissue in my abs, back, and legs. It gave my body some relief because it was receiving oxygen to breathe and my scars loosened up, thus correcting some of the tightness in my abs and back. Now I don't have such a leg length difference. The last time it was measured it was about an inch, and now I think it's even less than that.

At CSCIR, they didn't want to create more problems so they said, "Okay, sister, before we get you to one cane, or even allow you to think about this one cane business, we have to get your back straighter." I went through all the phases there: walker, crutches, two standard canes.

When it came time for me to practice with one cane though, my physical therapist did not allow it. She wanted to discharge me. She said it was too hard. I didn't have the strength. She wanted me to do only fitness for six months then she would reevaluate me to see if I was strong enough. This was very upsetting with all the progress I was making. She got on the phone with my rehabilitation doctor of eleven years and they agreed; it was unsafe. This doctor had also predicted I would never walk without any walking device.

In addition, my doctor of eleven years stopped writing my prescriptions for physical therapy. I had to find a new physical therapist, a new facility, and a new doctor who wanted to support me. I tried to explain that walking with one cane was supposed to be hard in the beginning. After all, when I first started using a walker from a wheelchair it was the same way—unstable, unsafe. I had to think about my steps and was out of breath. I had less energy. Now the walker and forearm crutches are easier. Taking steps is no longer something I have to think about. It's more natural, innate. I'm not there with one cane.

Healing is a process! Miracles don't happen overnight. They can, but it seems to me that spinal cord injury doesn't know years. We should never give up hope to recover. We can still be healed.

Throughout the years I have marveled at some healthcare professionals who go into the field but are so concerned with research and science that it seems to override their common sense. I have often felt that I was just the "patient" in physical therapy, and that my needs, wishes, and care were not the main concern. Whenever a physical therapist or doctor has made me feel that way, it did not feel good. Since their job is to help others, they should be more open to hearing suggestions from patients.

We cannot ignore the fact that walking after spinal cord injury is not easy. We also have to take into account that although we have not found a cure, there is a lot we cannot explain about spinal cord injury, such as how some nerves and muscles heal below the level of injury. There have been explanations that my injury is "incomplete." But on my medical reports from the University of Michigan, it clearly reads that I was diagnosed with an L2-L3 *complete* injury.

Why do we need a scientific explanation? Rather than just say this is a modern-day miracle? If we say it is a miracle, I guess that means anything can happen. But we don't want to say that because we might give someone "false hope." I ask you: what is wrong with "false hope"? I think it's better than no hope.

In healthcare, one of our major focuses is safety. I agree that you have to make sure a patient can get up off the floor before you approve them to walk with crutches or a cane. I understand that we have to be careful for ice, careful for falls. I have done all of those things. On icy days, I take out my walker to avoid that. I take safety precautions. I know my limits and measures.

I've also heard that we have to make sure you stand up straight. We have to make sure your posture is good if we allow you to practice with one cane, because twenty years from now you may damage other muscle groups by not walking properly. But I'm not concerned with twenty years from now. I'm concerned with right now. If I am always so careful because I want to be so safe that I never try anything new, even in physical therapy with someone assisting me, is it better for me to stay confined to a wheelchair?

The Power of Imagination

Going from paralyzed to walking does not look good. When I got up on a walker, I had a hip hike. I was slow. It is the same way with moving to one cane. The sad thing is that it has often been a struggle for me to get support when I have pushed myself in physical therapy. No matter how good and freeing it feels to walk with the least amount of assistance, I have always felt the creation of fear around doing it.

If your spine is broken, the messages your brain sends do not always work. For example, if I tell my leg to move, my brain will send that message to my spinal cord, and if there is nerve damage my brain may be saying it but my leg may not be doing it because of the nerve damage. The nerves attach to the muscles, and if the nerves cannot do it, the muscles typically can't. These two entities seem to work hand-in-hand.

I remember the best advice I ever got from Barb, my physical therapist at Barnum Rehabilitation, when I was in high school. She said, "We are going to do this exercise, or try it. Even if you are not able to do it, try. Try to do it. With all your strength. Imagine you are able to do it. Even if you don't see your leg moving or lifting up when you perform the exercise, the nerves and muscles are still activating. Imagine you are doing it."

I listened to Barb. We would do this repeatedly, and over time the muscle started to move and we saw muscle activity during the exercises. If the nerves have damage and the muscles don't want to work, but you train those muscles, they do start to move. You just have to imagine it, practice it, see it, and not give up! *Imagination is a powerful tool.* When you imagine it you are having faith. *"Faith is the realization of what is hoped for and evidence of things not seen"* (Hebrews 11:1).

That is why physical therapy and exercise are so important. That is why training your body to walk, even if you need three trainers beside you moving your legs for you, is so important. If you train your body and teach your mind to do it, eventually you can start to get some return. It may be slow and you may not go climbing to the top of Mt. Everest anytime soon, but you can recover.

Being injured so badly at sixteen helped me learn a lot about medicine and in some ways made me my own doctor. I learned how to listen to my own inner voice when I needed to. That healthy voice, that intuitive voice, comes from God. It speaks to me, teaches me how to take instruction, who to listen to, who not to listen to, and how to handle opposing beliefs.

From the beginning I had faith in Jesus, and I never let any dim prediction determine my destiny. It makes me sad how patients who have not known better have listened to the attitudes of defeat. Stayed home, believed they could not progress, and remained confined to a wheelchair. Today I do everything from a walking standpoint. My wheelchair is tucked away in my closet daily. I try to use it minimally.

In the community, I only take it out if I'm going somewhere with very long walking distances like an airport. I'm now able to take my crutches into the mall while shopping and into hospitals too, so it is rare that I take the wheelchair out. I have stopped putting a wheelchair in and out of my car. And 2011 is the first year I took some steps in physical therapy with no walking device, with a physical therapist beside me; 2012 was the first year I was able to use a treadmill with only one arm and not two. I'm now practicing with Figure 8 splints, something athletes wear for a minor sprain.

I don't have time for naysayers. I see how far I've come with faith and a lot of hard work, and I rejoice!

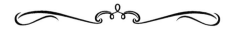

Chapter 5

Some Quick Tips on How I Heal

He strode into my hospital room one day, brushing past my mother. She must've been petrified. After all, English was her second language. She was mad, but all her strength couldn't stop him from what he was about to do: tell her precious daughter, her youngest, she would never walk again—and would have to live in a wheelchair for the rest of her life.

"You'll never walk again," he proclaimed. "Your accident…it…it…was just too bad." He said the words quickly, almost blurting them just to get them out. Clearly, he had been arguing outside the door with my mother, who looked as if she wanted to throw him out the window!

He was just doing his job, or what he thought he was supposed to do: tell the bad news. He stood up tall in front of my bed, white coat, dutiful doctor and all. One would think that as a teenager I would've felt fear. He didn't know my spirit. Instead I yelled back "Yes I will!" in the same tone he gave me, as if I were throwing the dodge ball back. "You're not God!"

I don't know what angered me more, his trying to tell me what I would or wouldn't do or his disregard for my mother. Even at a young age, I was protective of my mother. After we exchanged a few more words and I convinced him that I wouldn't accept his proposal, he stormed out of the room.

om had a strong faith too, and I know that helped me. She told me I would walk again. I believed her. This doctor tried hard to tell me I wouldn't. He wasn't among my life-saving team of surgeons. They never would have said that to me. He was just a random internal medicine doctor who worked on the floor doing his rounds that day. He had our floor more than once because I remember seeing him a few times, but I can't even remember his name. Just goes to show the impression he left on me.

When you are trying to get well, your goal is to recover and heal. Why is it that after spinal cord injury some health professionals tell you that you'll be limited and confined to a wheelchair?

With no regard for miracles, some health professionals give a diagnosis according to science and the latest research—

and nothing more. Oftentimes some stubborn ones, like the doctor in the story above, act as if they know everything. But I am stubborn too. Some tried to defeat my dream. But I never cared. I held onto what I believed, even if I did get treated like I was crazy. I held onto what God told me. I would walk. And I did.

Remember the story in John 5 where a paralytic man is healed by the pool at Bethesda. He waited thirty-eight years!

My physician of eleven years told me it would be hard for me to walk with no support. I told her my goal was to at least be mobile and get around everywhere with one cane. She said it was "possible" but not "probable." I countered that it was something I believed was very highly likely. I never accepted her proposition. I'm working toward achieving my goal.

Here are some ways I have gotten better:

- Daily prayer
- Exercise/physical therapy
- Keeping logs (Exercise logs can be great. I've even kept logs on what percentage of the day I use a wheelchair. Track your progress!)
- Keeping food diaries
- Listening to my doctors but not neglecting my own "doctor" within, my intuition.

PRAYER: I talk to God daily. I talk to Him while at the gym on the walking machines. I talk to Him while at the grocery store shopping. I talk to Him as I'm in class preparing to teach, and I hear from Him while I'm teaching too because He knows I need to. It can be stressful. And if I stay quiet enough, I can hear from Him when I'm under pressure.

I sometimes read Bible verses and short prayers in the morning. If I can commit to just fifteen minutes a day of doing this, it really helps me. I write letters to God in the morning or at night in my journals. We speak through worship and prayer songs, when I really feel the Holy Spirit. I especially talk to Him at night before I go to bed, when it's quiet. That is when I can hear Him best.

Prayer helps rejuvenate my mind. Prayer can be a way of processing information. We can talk to God about anything: our worries, our hopes, our good and bad days, our feelings toward our family, where we want to be five years from now. We can tell Him how we truly feel; He knows our hearts. We can say prayers before meals and before we go to bed. We can thank Him throughout the day via a powerful form of prayer—praise.

We can read the Psalms and study the Bible. We can say the Lord's Prayer. We can light a candle. We can talk to Him in the car on our way to work. Prayer comes in many forms. It's free. It's easy to access. We can never run out of things to pray about.

My PICU nurse Regina gave me the best advice that anyone ever gave me. "No matter what, keep your eyes on Jesus," she said. "No matter what, just keep your eyes on Him. Don't take your eyes off Jesus. Everything will work out." Regina was the first medical professional to tell me I would walk again.

She put the poem I wrote titled "God" in a plaque for me on my birthday while I was still in the hospital. She also bought my first Bible. I've had that same Bible for nineteen years now.

I still have my poem "God" in a plaque on the mantel in my living room.

Regina is in heaven now. She was diagnosed with cancer in 2012, and within a year she was gone. In my last conversation with her son, Glenn, his strength and attitude amazed me. Since my accident I've been blessed to have him as a good friend.

Talking to God, having that relationship, having that connection, focusing my thoughts on Him—is imperative for me. Prayer is the pathway that connects us to the heavens. No prayer is unheard, although they may seem unanswered. We have to trust that God has a plan, even when we cannot make sense of things. In time the answers will reveal themselves.

Prayer helps us see clearly. Prayer can be a weapon. Prayer can be an affirmation. The power of prayer is infinite. Simply say "Amen." It is one of the greatest gifts in the world.

EXERCISE/PHYSICAL THERAPY: Exercise or physical therapy is something you should be doing **at least** a few times a week. If you do not need physical therapy, exercise is still priceless. Find a physical therapist or trainer who can design a safe but challenging program for you.

"Get up close and personal with yourself, get to know yourself," Dr. David B. Agus writes in his No. 1 *New York Times* bestseller, *The End of Illness*. Dr. Agus continues on how to prevent disease: "Americans don't move around enough, most people go to the gym for an hour, go back to their office, sit at their desk jobs for hours, and they think that is enough....Every hour you should move, even if for no reason, get away from your desk, find a reason to get up."

What if you're spinal-cord injured? What if you can't get up easily? What if you can't stand? What if you can't walk? What if you can't even sit for long periods of time or get out of a wheelchair without someone assisting you?

I believe any movement is good movement to start. Whether it's a transfer from your wheelchair to your bed, or using the hand-cycling machine at physical therapy, or standing for several minutes at a time in a standing frame, it gets your heart pumping, your blood flowing, and your body moving. As you train your body to move with help, and eventually without help—to transfer, to sit for longer periods, to stand, to walk, whatever you are able to do—it gets stronger. Over time you can become more independent.

Just be safe. When I practice with one cane, I'm usually with a physical therapist. When I'm doing it at home, I try my best to be safe. I may stay closer to walls and counters.

It's crucial for someone with paralysis to move because they don't do it easily on a daily basis. I believe it's even more important for us to get up. Dr. Agus's advice applies to all of us, those with and without physical challenges. For those who cannot move their hands, feet, or fingers even, it can be much harder to get up or even feel motivated to move.

In his book *The Omni Diet: Lose up to 12 LBS in 2 weeks* Dr. Daniel Amen says, "When you are ill or in the hospital, your energy demands go up four times and it is protein your body uses as fuel to repair itself. *And muscle is your protein reserve.* Studies show that the less muscle you have the less chance you have of a full recovery."

Dr. Amen continues: "When researchers from Tufts University taught elderly people in nursing homes how to do simple strength training exercises they gained muscles, improved mobility and became less frail and gained more independence, all in a few short weeks. Muscles respond incredibly quickly to strength training at every age. Strength training just a couple days a week can even reverse muscle loss."

My feet are weak because my S1/S2 nerves still have some damage. I can push my feet down, but it's harder to pull my feet up against gravity. Throughout the day I'm wearing AFOs (ankle braces) to assist my walking. But Dr. Susan Harkema, a research leader in the field, says, "Twenty years of study in humans has shown that the spinal cord has its own sophisticated nervous system that helps it recall how to move."

Recovery depends on many different factors: your level of injury, the nature of your injury, and your *faith*. Exercise and movement not only improve health but can help you regain function. The number one factor is *you*.

<u>KEEPING LOGS</u>: Exercise logs are a great way to track your progress. It's inspiring to see how far you've come. As you increase minutes on the bicycle, treadmill, elliptical, or other various machines, you can see your duration progress. It's also nice to see your number of exercise repetitions go up.

I've kept logs on the amount of time daily I spend using a wheelchair. I would record the number of minutes I sat throughout the day and the number of hours I was awake and walking on crutches or other walking devices. Then at the end of the day I would divide the total amount of time I spent in the wheelchair by the amount of time I spent walking, and I would multiply it times a hundred to get a decimal and round it off to get a percentage.

I remember how much recording helped. I was able to keep using a wheelchair under 20 percent of the day by doing this. I began to decrease the amount of time I sat by paying attention to when I did and what times of the day I was tired, and then doing my best to prevent it.

FOOD DIARIES: I've kept a food diary. Spinal cord injury not only affects your limbs, it can also affect your overall health and digestive system. It can cause constipation or even irritable bowel syndrome if you don't eat properly with nutritional foods. Both soluble fiber (fruit, beans, peas, and oats) and insoluble fiber (greens, nuts, seeds, beans, and skins of grains) are essential. Gradually increase your fiber intake.

Keeping a food diary really helped me learn what types of foods I could and could not eat. Over time I became healthier and it seemed even the foods that once bothered me became easier to eat again because I learned what foods my body could handle. Mainly, greasier foods or foods cooked with oils and spices would sometimes bother me. But after a while I no longer had to keep a food diary. However, I still had to accompany the right food with plenty of exercise!

FOLLOW YOUR INTUITION: As I mentioned before, listen to and respect your doctors, but don't neglect your own "doctor within." You know that inner voice. We all have it, the one that screams at you to take a left or right when you are lost and driving the wrong way. Your intuition is powerful, and it has something to say. Pay attention to it. Do research on the Internet. Learn about your health. Know your body. Trust your doctor, but know what is best for you. Medical decisions should be mutual and also feel comfortable to you.

These are some ways I get better from spinal cord injury. I believe these principles can apply to all of us. Prayer and exercise and getting to know our bodies can help us all.

Writing and Reflection:

Here are five additional points you can reflect upon, similar to the ones described above. In each paragraph, think more about how you can practice these attitudes or activities. What can you do to accomplish them? How will it help you live a healthier life? Think of this as a homework assignment, but you are also the teacher. Take notes. Put your answers in a journal. Assess yourself.

- Prayer – How can I get better at this? Can I cut the radio out while driving? Can I spend time in the quiet and give up the television or social media for a little bit of time with the Lord?
- Exercise – How much of this am I doing? How can I improve in this area? Can I keep a schedule as if it were a job?
- Determination – Is anything bogging me down? Have I lost belief in myself? Or zest for life? Are there any areas of defeat? (Try filling those with healthy thoughts about yourself that speak positivity. Read Scripture. Say prayers of affirmation. It will make a difference.)

- Outlets (Friendships/Family/Groups) – How can I get more support? Am I extending myself? Can I join a support group? A swim club? A local church? Where can I feel acceptance?
- Be Proactive in Your Health – Do I keep a folder with medical reports? Am I aware of the side effects of medication? (Know about yourself!)

Chapter 6

"Faith of a Million Dollars!"

While living in the apartment with my sisters during my senior year of high school, I used to listen to a live radio broadcast of people who would call in nightly for prayer. The program, NightVision, was broadcast on Christian radio station WMUZ/103.5 FM in Michigan. Run by Pastor George Bogle and his wife, by that time the program had already been on the radio for more than twenty years. I sometimes heard people call from places such as St. Louis or other parts of the United States.

The program was especially helpful because this was the period when I was abandoned by my best friends in high school.

So I would turn on the radio station to find some encouragement. It worked.

People asked for help with their finances. They prayed about sicknesses or for healing of their loved ones who were ill. I even heard a truck driver request prayer for safety while driving on icy roads. Listening to others' concerns and having the opportunity to pray for them with Pastor Bogle took my mind off what I was going through. I've heard before that when you're in trouble, it's good to pray for others to get the focus off yourself. The advice was, "Anytime you want to stop feeling sorry for yourself, start praying for someone else." It has a healing effect on all of us.

Regularly, this program would come on from 12-2 a.m. When Pastor Bogle was through, another pastor came on the air from 2-3 a.m. I couldn't always stay awake for the following pastor's program. Often I would wake up in the morning to the radio playing beside my head. These programs calmed my emotions at a time when I really needed it, shortly after my accident.

The second pastor's program had the same format. People called in for live prayer and he would pray for them too. One night I was doing the usual—listening to the radio before I fell asleep in bed. I couldn't stay up for the second program. Still attending physical therapy and praying to walk, I had been particularly frustrated that day.

Suddenly I awakened from a deep sleep, as if someone literally shook me. But when I looked to see who woke me, no one was there. Houda and Sandy were sound asleep. The second pastor was prophesying, as he would sometimes do. It was well after two o'clock by this time, and when I woke up I heard him say: "There is someone listening. You have a problem with your back.

There is some sort of problem of…I'm not sure what happened or how…but something with your back is all I keep feeling. God wants you to know—He's going to build a bridge. God is just going to build a bridge for you. He is going to take you above and beyond what anyone could ever think would happen for you! The Lord is just going to build a bridge."

He kept repeating that, speaking in this manner for a few minutes. It was amazing. Instantly I knew that message was for me. Especially with the way I woke up. I called the broadcast before he was even finished prophesying. Surprisingly, I got through the telephone line and told him my situation and how I was upset that I still could not walk. It had been at least a year since my accident, but I believed his message was for me and I wanted to make sure of that.

First he confirmed that the message *was* for me. He said again, "The Lord is just going to build a bridge. He will take you above and beyond what anyone ever thought could happen for you. He's just going to build a bridge."

"Okay!" I said happily. But I told him I was still very upset that I couldn't walk after my spinal cord injury. I told him that I had the faith to walk and I knew God wanted to heal me, but I couldn't understand why it was taking so long.

"For your miracle, you need a lot of faith," he explained. "For example, how much faith do you need to get one dollar?"

"Not a lot," I said.

"Not much faith, right? It's only one dollar."

"Right."

"To get ten dollars, you need a little more faith, right?"

"Sure, a little more than that."

"But it's feasible to get ten dollars, isn't it? I mean, it's not too difficult to get ten dollars, right?"

"Right," I agreed.

"But to get *a million dollars*, how much faith do you need? You need a lot of faith, right? How much faith do you need to get a million dollars?"

"More, you need a lot more faith, pastor," I said, laughing.

"*You need the faith of that to get a million dollars!*" At first when he said that, I was taken aback. But he explained, "It's because it needs to grow; have patience. You need the faith of that to get a million dollars, then you will walk!"

As he explained it to me, I understood more fully. I don't remember the pastor's name but his message stayed with me. He said my faith needed to grow and that my faith would grow. As it did, I would continue to get better.

Healing Starts in the Mind

I share this story of the pastor who prophesied my healing at eighteen for anyone who may need a big miracle in their own life. Your miracle may be completely different from my own, but it's something that requires a lot of faith. God wants to stretch your faith! At the time, I couldn't understand why my miracle was not happening, and he likened my faith to walk again to the faith needed to get a million dollars—because it's hard to do! It made sense and was easy to understand.

I believe that healing starts in the mind. It is a process. It doesn't happen overnight. Not that it can't. Spinal cord injury recovery can take years. As the pastor said, our faith needs to grow. Back then I thought I would be healed within two years.

The sad reality is that spinal cord injury usually doesn't work like that. If I look back at the pastor's prediction, I realize that is how I have healed—year by year. I am still making progress.

God had to heal some things within in order for my healing on the outside to begin. "Sometimes it takes physical illness to restore the heart's ability to heal," is a quote I once read by someone who signed anonymously. I have found this to be true.

Conditions can be side effects of broken hearts or stress. People see life for what it is while suffering, because it allows us to call out to God in our weakness. In our reaching out to Him, we start to feel better on the inside. It becomes evident on the outside too. I keep a blog at http://zinahermez.wordpress.com. People write to me with comments in response to my articles. I would like to share some of the comments on one of my posts.

FROM MY BLOG

A man from Atlanta, Georgia. Married with two children, well-to-do with a beautiful family and thriving career, sadly suffered from paralysis after a tumor removal from his spine.

Over the last 2 years my body has been literally destroyed. I can no longer go for my daily run. I can no longer easily go on business trips without my wife or caregiver, or pick up my share of the load in our growing business to give my loyal partner a well-deserved break. I have been perpetually ill and just got out of the hospital last night after an 8 day stint with a serious case of pneumonia. This is my third hospital stay since Thanksgiving. My 9th in 2 years. In exchange

I have discovered a closer and much more meaningful, deeper relationship with God and his son Jesus Christ. My marriage has substantially improved and I am now home to interact with our 10 year old twin daughters. I am able to share with them spiritual knowledge gained that I would never have known absent my paralysis. The bible says that those who suffer as Jesus did will be "Co heirs of his Kingdom in Heaven." Much of my peace comes from now knowing there is at least a chance for me!

—Pete

FROM MY BLOG
My response to him
Hi Pete,

Sorry to hear you just got out of the hospital, again. Everything you said about being a different person now by having more time to be at home since your paralysis, and teach your daughters makes so much sense. It seems sometimes, when we have hardship, we get to really see life for what it is. We appreciate more, become closer to God as we call on Him. My accident happened when I was just sixteen, so it was interesting to read the difference in how someone changed by their injury as being an adult. I know God is with you and loves you and your family, and I'm sure all of the hospital visits are discouraging. But hang in there. I believe you'll be alright. I'm praying for your recovery.

—Zina

The reason I wanted to share this is because Pete's story reminds me of the preciousness in calling out to God. Pete had lost, as I did, physically, but in turn he gained a greater gift, the Lord Jesus Christ. I think it's beautiful that he is able to recognize that. What happened to him as an adult transformed him into an even better father and husband. That is the miracle! It helped me see how much I've been given.

Susan Taylor says, "Seeds of faith are always within us; sometimes it takes a crisis to nourish and encourage their growth." When you've gone through something tragic, you can feel a deeper sense of appreciation for life. Don't get me wrong. There will be days when you won't feel so high, but resilience is key. It's how you bounce back. You're okay as long as you don't stay stuck in "woe is me." That pattern is not very healthy.

Every day is a gift. Jesus taught me that. And if I take a look at what I've endured, it's nothing compared to what He went through for me. Every day brings hope, love, and the opportunity to heal and experience the beauty of life.

How about you? What do you do when you are having a bad day? What do you do when you have no one to talk to? Try praying—talk to God. He wants to have a relationship with you. He wants to be your best friend.

Get out in the community. Make new friends. Try remedies that work. About a year and a half ago, I joined an online Christian writers' group where I met authors who mentored me through the Internet. My life changed again for the better. Through classes, webinars, and friendly emails I've been encouraged to write. I started my blog to help cope with my spinal cord injury, in hopes of helping others. It has been therapeutic and given me great relief.

My recovery—along with so many others who are going through challenges—is a process. We have to be patient. I am in no way suggesting it is easy; it is not for me. There are setbacks, there are failures. But we must not give up faith to get well because it's never too late!

I believe God designs things His way for His own purposes and orchestrates things for reasons that we cannot understand. That is what trust in God is about. Not questioning. Just trusting. It's hard to do, believe me. I have to work at it too. Could you imagine if we practiced it more? *How much better would our lives be?* He knows what's best for us, and He understands why things happen as they do. I am not one of those who believe that God deliberately does bad things to me. I believe His love is unconditional. Yet I do know that suffering exists.

In 2009 I bought a book titled *The Promise: God's Purpose and Plan for When Life Hurts* by Father Jonathan Morris, a religious news analyst and commentator who served as an advisor to Mel Gibson during the making of *The Passion of the Christ*.

He discusses three back-to-back tragedies: the Asian tsunami, the Pakistan earthquake, and the hurricane in New Orleans. He teaches about the coexistence of God and suffering. His book helped console me in rough times. "Jesus is in our corner, in our suffering he's in our room," he writes. "I have always felt that. In all the fear and anguish, I've always felt God with me, holding my hand, leading me, telling me the next step to take, the next move.

"A person who has suffered deeply and triumphed is now a better person. Precisely because of pain and suffering, his life story is better. He has forged character; he has become more human." Here is a question from Father Jon's book we can all think about: "How can I transform my suffering into a springboard for personal growth?" Our suffering will never be rational or make sense, but what can we do to better our life despite circumstances that are not so bright? At times I am frustrated with not being able to just get up and walk freely, without crutches. Then I always remind myself of how blessed I am to be alive and able to walk at all.

I remember the doctor who predicted that I would never walk again. Then I focus on ways I have gotten better, things I can do physically now that I couldn't before. For example, I've only been able to grocery shop on my crutches in the last couple of years. For many years I went into the market and only shopped with a wheelchair.

The same is true of taking out the garbage. I couldn't do that before because I didn't have enough balance to walk on forearm crutches and carry a garbage bag at the same time. Maybe it was the fear that the weight from the bag would pull me down and I'd lose my balance and fall to the ground. Now I can. I can take out garbage while walking and standing up. I try to focus on these good things, these positive things I have learned how to do. It helps the stuff I can't do not seem so bad.

Greater than grocery shopping or taking out garbage on crutches is the fact that I have made peace. As the Bible states in Philippians 4:7, *"Then the peace of God that surpasses all understanding will guard your hearts and minds in Christ Jesus."* I am at peace with my life. Although I do not accept my limitations, I am thankful for what I can do—but that does not mean I don't push forward. I still work relentlessly and plan for how to achieve my goal of walking with one cane or less.

When I've been asked how I am content in what others would deem a bleak situation, I try to put value on the journey by explaining that I've gone from paralyzed to walking. When you cannot move your legs and then gain the miracle of being able to walk, it is priceless. I may not be quite at the "faith of a million dollars" yet, but I believe I'm close!

Chapter 7

Going Out into the Real World

"Are you okay?" my student Angelika asked, concerned.

"Sure, why wouldn't I be?" I responded, but I knew why she asked.

"Oh, it's just…because you're sitting today." Her voice got lower, almost not claiming what she had just said.

As I rolled my wheelchair to the front of the classroom I assured her, "Oh yeah, I brought my wheelchair. I take it out sometimes on really bad snow days. I'm fine. It's okay."

Angelika's face lit up. That was more important to me than how I felt. Her ease meant more than my unease at that moment. She went to sit in her chair as we prepared to start grammar class.

t he way I felt inside that day was completely opposite. I don't like taking my wheelchair to work. I can count on my hands how many times I've taken it to class. I'm always walking with forearm crutches. When people see me in the wheelchair they get surprised, even concerned, and so they ask. It's no big deal. I'm glad they care.

In Michigan we have harsh winters. That day in early 2013 when Angelika inquired about my wheelchair was the worst it had been in a couple of years. While walking to my car that morning down the ramp outside my apartment, I was unaware that my right crutch hit an ice patch. We were in the midst of a winter snowstorm that morning. My crutch gave out and my body twisted as I fell to the ground on my right hip. Thankfully, I was okay.

My neighbor Jay saw me outside and came out quickly to help get me off the ground and back inside. I'm the type who likes to think I can do everything anyone else can, but this was a wakeup call for me to take more precaution in the winter, especially when leaving for work in the mornings.

I try to use the wheelchair minimally. As I mentioned in a previous chapter, I had no choice in college but to put the wheelchair in and out of my car several times a day. The feeling of throwing my lightweight crutches in the car is freeing to me.

Several minutes prior to Angelika's inquiry, my director also asked how I felt. "If I throw my back out and need to bring my cane, it's the same thing," she said, trying to make me feel better. Even though I never told her I don't like to take the wheelchair out, I think she can sense that. Everyone can. I appreciated her trying to comfort me, but really it's not the same. I would much rather walk with one cane than use a wheelchair.

For one, it's much easier to put in and out of a car. My wheelchair is a manual one. I've never had a power wheelchair. Those are heavier. A person with a power chair typically needs someone to drive them around like a family member, caregiver, or transportation company. The power chair is very heavy and I never wanted one. I wanted to keep my upper body strong. I would rather maintain good strength than let a wheelchair do all the work for me.

Nevertheless, I still have to stand at my car and pop each wheel off my manual wheelchair and put them in the back seat. Then fold the wheelchair down and put in the base of the chair. And vice versa; when I arrive at my destination I have to put the wheelchair back together all over again after I pull it out.

I got my director's point though, and it was nice she was trying to comfort me in my discomfort. "Oh God, I hope I never see that," I said, trying to lighten things up in reference to her cane. I'm more sensitive to people having trouble walking because I've had so much.

I think this is about acceptance for me. I've come far, maybe not as far as I'd like, but walking with nothing is a big goal considering the injuries I had. Still, I believe it's possible because with God *all things are possible*. It's no fun taking a wheelchair out, but I feel grateful that I can put it in and out of the car. I never want to become comfortable—just give up and not progress toward getting better. Have you ever felt that? Has it ever been hard for you to accept something different about you?

A Gift for Teaching

I've been teaching at the Language Center International for three years now. I have students from various backgrounds and cultures, ranging from doctors to even pastors. Some are from Europe, some from Asia, and some from the Middle East. All of my students want to further their careers or earn additional degrees, and their goal is to better their English.

I also do one-to-one teaching for a global language-training company called Global LT. The two part-time jobs make my teaching career full-time. I teach English as a second language to mostly engineers who are living in the US temporarily on work assignments with their families. Global LT has contracts with automotive corporations, and they send me to teach English at these companies.

Most of my students are at the Nissan Technical Center North America. A division of Nissan North America, it is the research and development center in the US, with about one thousand employees working in the building. There are two assembly plants in the US, one in Smyrna, Tennessee, and one in Canton, Mississippi.

The Smyrna plant is the largest with a total of around ten thousand employees, my students said. Since Nissan is a Japanese company, most of my students here have been Japanese, though I've had students from Mexico and even Brazil at Nissan too. I've been doing this work for nearly six years and I don't speak a word of Japanese. All of my students are able to speak English; they are just at different levels. Some are at a beginner level, some intermediate. On occasion I get a student who is a little more advanced. They are able to communicate, but they need some assistance.

For example, verb tense can be problematic for English language learners as well as prepositions, vocabulary, etc. Simply expressing yourself can be a challenge when you are from another country. I help them with overall English as well as with presentations or reports for work, if they need someone to proofread or assistance with writing. I even help them with something as simple as calling a telephone company about a bill.

When you include all the grading and lesson planning, I work as much as anyone with a nine-to-five position. For Global LT, we are sometimes required to teach in the student's home, or they may prefer to meet in a public place such as a library. We try our best to accommodate them.

Going to a student's home has not always been easy. It was a struggle to get into a student's home one particular night on a teaching assignment. There were three staircases to get into his house—about ten steps to get inside the old burgundy brick building's door, and then two additional sets of stairs to reach my student's condominium.

I wasn't expecting all those stairs when I arrived, but I held onto the railing with one hand and used a crutch in the other hand. The railing on the second set of steps was shaky so I tried not to lean on it. It took about five extra minutes. I was embarrassed and I apologized, but my student assured me it was okay and that he didn't mind.

It's my own insecurity, this shortcoming. We all have them but mine are visible. God has given me students who accept me, and that is a blessing. No one ever expects to live with a physical challenge. It's not something we foresee as a child. It's not how we envision our lives. It's definitely not something we expect.

I've learned to see my challenge as a part of life. Suffering is sometimes inevitable. I've learned that heaven is the only perfect place, with golden streets and pearl gates, massive choirs of angels singing praises. I've read books about people who've visited there. Call me naïve, but I believe. I don't recall heaven at the scene of my accident or in my hospital bed, but I felt this profound sense of peace. In the midst of crisis, chaos, and catastrophe, God was watching over me.

God is still working matters out to my advantage. He always sends the right people to help me. At the Nissan Technical Center, the walk from the parking lot to the door of the building is kind of far, even from the handicapped spots. Wes, the grounds supervisor, always advises me to park in the front of the building. Although no one is allowed to park there, he told me to just throw up my handicap sticker, no problem. He has alerted security that if they see my car, it is me parking there. It's a short distance to walk to the doors, so it is nice that he offered this.

I only take advantage of that when it's icy outside, or if the rain is coming down hard. Whenever Wes sees me walking in from the parking lot, he asks me why I didn't park up front. I tell him it's because I like the exercise and I'm trying to walk as best I can. I want to be like everyone else.

Some of the ladies there ask about my progress and tell me how good I'm doing at walking and how proud they are of me. I've told them my story and that I was paralyzed. A few of them get really encouraged and happy when they see me walking. So I try to do my best.

I can't help but notice how sometimes doors fly open as soon as I walk up to them. People seem to be aware of my inability. It's not every day you see a woman walking into a large corporation with forearm crutches. It's nice that people like to help. I sometimes get stares when I walk in there. But almost always I get smiles and friendly hellos.

I can feel when I am being watched though. I walk with confidence but with forearm crutches. That is not common in our society. So much is based on how we look. So much is focused on our appearance.

Because Nissan is a global corporation, people come from all over to visit. Various suppliers come from in and out of state wanting to land a contract. I notice different accents and can tell when someone is from Tennessee, or even from as far away as England. People sometimes ask why I am on crutches out of curiosity. I explain to them about my accident and tell them how God saved me.

Oftentimes they smile and nod their head, impressed. They may share some words. Some I feel are studying me, trying to figure out what is wrong. Others simply glance. It's human nature.

I sometimes have to drag myself out of bed to start early in the morning. My body is kind of stiff, and to be there by 8 a.m. I have to get up around 6:30. I get there though because it is my job and I enjoy teaching. I have always supported myself. It is my income. It is how I make a living. And for the most part all of my students, at the Language Center and Global LT, have been very nice to me.

Writing = Manifestation

The reason I majored in English was not primarily to teach but to write. I worked for my brother's small construction company as a secretary while I was getting through classes at the community college. At Oakland University, I worked on campus doing student jobs while taking classes and going to the Recreational Center to work out. First I worked in the physical therapy department for ten months. Then I worked in the international students' office for a year, but it helped me to pay for my apartment rent and tuition, classes, books, and things like that.

I was receiving grants because I did not have any financial assistance with school. The government gave me the PELL grant and considered me independent. I had to take out student loans to pay for what the grants didn't cover.

In December 2005, before I started with Global LT and the Language Center International, I began running tutoring services. That was my first "teaching job," and I was twenty-seven years old. I started contracting my own students and servicing them for one- to two-hour lessons, sometimes one or more times a week. I worked with all ages, kindergarten through adults. I taught English, reading, writing, and tutored junior high and high school students in math. I did website development and helped some businesses with proofreading and editing. I also homeschooled kids in geometry, biology, or whatever subject was needed. I started my own small business!

I did this for a couple of years, but when I started with Global LT in October 2007 I did both at the same time for a while. Then it got to be a lot of work for me so I stayed mainly with Global LT. The busiest I ever got was up to about twenty hours a week tutoring students of my own.

The likelihood of someone with a spinal cord injury finding work is a low 26 percent, compared with 81 percent (almost three times higher) for the non-injured. I feel blessed to have always had employment.

Writing is also now a part of my life, and it has changed my life. I've kept a journal on and off for many years, often writing in the mornings. I write letters addressed to God; I know He can hear me. I have shared some of my diary entries at sixteen and seventeen years old in this book.

I launched my blog in June 2012, and you can find it at http://zinahermez.wordpress.com. You can also see my website at www.zinahermez.com. You are welcome to visit and can even subscribe to my blog. You will get an update each time I write a new article, if you would like to stay connected. I write to encourage and share with others, with or without spinal cord injury.

Writing provides manifestation. When I can see my thoughts, I can sort them out. This especially helps if I am confused about something and need to find a solution. I have advised students to keep a journal over the years. Sometimes people ask what made me want to write. To me, it's no wonder that I wrote a book. It has been a remedy all my life.

In Louise Desalvo's book *Writing as a Way of Healing: How Telling Our Story Transforms Our Lives*, she asks what hurts us. She says that is what we should write about. I agree. It may not make the problem go away, but it is medically proven that writing improves the neuro-pathways of the brain. What is your pain that we cannot see? What are you afraid to write? Tap into that place. Write it down, if only for yourself. It is a form of therapy.

I am excited to have writing as a career now. I've always written, even when I was in the second grade. I'll never forget winning my first story contest in elementary school. I won a few. My teacher was so proud she designed a nice booklet for me made out of colorful construction paper that contained all my stories. It was such an accomplishment.

The first loss I ever experienced was losing that book. When I couldn't find it, I searched the basement tirelessly for two hours. It was my first heartbreak.

At sixteen in the hospital I wrote after my accident. Hooked up to machines with a breathing tube down my throat, the first few weeks I *had* to write. It was the **only way** to communicate; I couldn't talk. I still have all my notes of black marker scribbles on white and yellow cutouts from hospital flyer sheets. They are saved in my closet in a big bag with every word on every card that every person ever wrote to me.

After the PICU, I wrote in Mott Children's upstairs. I wrote letters to God each night. I poured out the sorrows, hopes, and dreams of my heart in the most difficult time in my life. I wrote through college, successes, heartbreaks, frustrations, or accomplishments. I kept thick journals, writing each night or when I felt the urge. I jotted down my emotions and thoughts. Again, the reason I majored in English was not to teach, it was to write. Finally, I'm achieving my heart's dream.

Threads of a Tapestry

I sit in the classroom sometimes and glance at my room full of students one by one, thinking *how did I get here?* It is surreal. I feel accomplished. It's interesting, but I always knew I would teach.

I flash back to that day in September 1994 when Mr. Peolke knocked on my classroom door to ask if he could have a word with me. I was still in my junior year at Harrison High School. What seemed to be a fresh start led to tragedy. When Mr. Peolke asked me to serve on the Multicultural/Multiracial Council that year, I gladly accepted. I excelled in the group for the short time I was able to participate. I impressed the teachers and staff with my comments about equality and how we are all the same. We should treat one another with the same respect. I was very involved. For the first time my life felt like it had meaning. Then, my accident.

Fast-forward nineteen years; now I sit in my classroom. I have overcome paralysis, my second miracle after life itself. I'm employed. I got through college. God promised me I would walk. I am walking. I stare at the students. I stare at the books laid all over my desk. I examine my students while they are taking a test. I have warned them not to cheat. My wheelchair is tucked away in my closet. I am using two forearm crutches and practicing with one cane in physical therapy. Not bad, something some health professionals said I would never do.

I look at my students and I marvel. *How did I get here?* That day, on October 18, 1994, I tried so desperately to get to school. I wanted to help. I wanted to be with my friends. I wanted to serve on the council. *I was on my way to school.* Sadly, I could not get there.

I was not able to fulfill my duty on the Multicultural/ Multiracial Council at school that year. But at thirty-five years old, God has given me a diversity panel of students of my own. It's interesting how that worked out.

I think back and wonder what made me become a teacher. Was it Mr. Naglik's history class in the seventh grade? I liked his passion for teaching. He was always animated and really involved as he stood up in the front of the room. He taught us about American history and world wars. He made learning history fun. *Did that lead me to minor in it?*

I think back to Mrs. Bahoura. I was pulled out of the regular class for an hour or two each day to work with a bilingual teacher in kindergarten and the first grade. I'm not sure if I "needed" her or if I was stereotyped as needing her by the school, because of my family's background. She said my problem was that I read too fast. It helped me to slow down. I'll never forget how nice she was to my mother. At that time, my mother spoke little English, and Mrs. Bahoura spoke Chaldean.

My mother came to all of my meetings, and Mrs. Bahoura would explain everything to her kindly. It was beautiful, watching the two of them. *Is that what inspired me to help families? Did Mrs. Bahoura encourage me to tutor all those years?*

I think back to Mrs. Honkola, my teacher in the third grade. All the kids loved her. Melissa Dean, my best friend and neighbor at the time, would talk about Mrs. Honkola and how awesome she was. Thinking back to Mrs. Honkola, it was not only what she said that demonstrated her love for children or her love for teaching. It was what she did. Each time I saw her walking down the hallway, she was always so excited to see me. I will never forget her in her matronly skirt.

It wasn't a simple gesture or smile, like some of the other teachers and administration staff would give. Not all of them even noticed the kids while walking by. Every time she saw me in that hallway she would stop in her tracks, look down at me with a big smile, and say, "Hi, Zina! How are you today?" As if seeing me made her day.

She waited for a genuine response. I remember how depressed I was when Melissa Dean later told me she had passed away from cancer. At first I didn't believe it was true. Melissa wasn't lying but she had to convince me. It was the first big sad news I had ever gotten at such a young age. Her memory has stayed with me. I ask myself, *Did Mrs. Honkola have something to do with my becoming a teacher?* I believe she did.

God professes things to us as children, even before we arrive. In Jeremiah 1:5, the word of the Lord came to the prophet saying, *"Before I formed you in the womb I knew you; before you were born I dedicated you, a prophet to the nations I appointed you."* God knows what we are supposed to do with our lives.

I flash back to my childhood best friend, Melissa, who lived across the street from me on Gramercy Court. Her mother, Mrs. Dean, was a writer. Daily she would click away at an old-fashioned typewriter, something you would probably find in an antique shop nowadays. She would sit in the living room for hours and just write. I always had a strong feeling I would do that one day. I just knew. I also had a feeling I would teach.

These people were role models that God sent into my life, writers and teachers and my angels in the hospital, Regina,

Dennis, my surgeons, and my mom. I see my teachers as people who led me to God's will for my life, His plan for me. Mr. Peolke, Mrs. Honkola, Mr. Naglik, and the others.

Every so often in our lives people come along who are meant to help us. They can simply point the way. Through a tragedy or difficulty of some kind, they can work as angels—they show up miraculously. Sometimes we don't even realize how much they actually helped until their work is done.

That is what so many have been to me: doctors, teachers, angels, and friends. I hope to be what these everyday heroes have been.

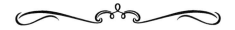

Chapter 8

Prepared for a Purpose

It's interesting, before my accident I would have these premonitions that came as warning signs or in thoughts, as if I were being given messages that something bad would happen to me. My sister Sandy and I shared a room with two twin beds upstairs in our home on Gramercy Court. You know that point you reach when you're on the brink—just about to fall asleep, on the verge, ready to fade into the calm?

I was hovering on that brink one night when suddenly *boom!* I heard a loud crashing noise. It lingered for a few moments. I could not move or open my eyes, just lie there. I could only wait for it to pass. It was very scary. When it stopped I was able to come out of it, and I immediately told my sister. It was the sound of a car crash. She was surprised. I don't think she really believed me, or maybe she was taken aback. This happened about a month before my accident. A message.

I used to think, *How do people ever do that? Like people who can't walk? How do they get around? How do they move?* I remembered a story I heard about a guy my family knew who woke up out of bed one day and couldn't move because of a rare disease that had progressed. He was only eighteen. *What if that happened to me? What if I could not move? What if I could not walk? I would get out of a wheelchair. I would do everything I could. I would never be stuck in a wheelchair!* These were my thoughts at about fifteen years old.

I remember hopping down our porch steps one time in my platform shoes to go out, thinking *this won't always be easy. I won't always feel so light on my feet.* I just knew I wouldn't always be able to do that. I don't know how I knew. I knew I would not always have such freedom in my body. I appreciated that I could move so freely.

Another time before my accident, I tumbled to the bathroom floor and tried to yell for my mom. I performed some strange sort of crawl on the cold tile floor, calling out "Mom." Just barely did my voice come out. It was a mumble. I was trying to get to the door but it was hard. Perhaps I fainted; I don't know. My mom could not hear me. She was downstairs. After some moments I was able to get up. This too was not long before my accident. It's as if I were being introduced to what was to come. A premonition.

For those few moments I was paralyzed. This incident happened another time as well, both incidents occurring shortly before my accident. Were these warning signs of my paralysis to come?

I've always been different. Not to say I've had a sixth sense. Maybe I could call it extra intuitive, or the ability to hear from God and the Holy Spirit. My accident was not the first time danger knocked on my door. Things had been tumultuous before the accident.

When I was eleven years old, I was babysitting my nephew Calvin. He is the oldest grandchild, the son of my eldest sister, Sue. He was only four years old at the time, and Sue had just had a baby girl, Megan, still under one year old. She needed to take Megan to the doctor so she asked me to come over and watch Calvin.

Calvin was standing on the porch crying when Sue, Megan, and my mom left for the doctor's appointment.

"Come on, Calvin, let's go inside," I told him. Finally I convinced him to go in. "Calvin, let's go play our game." We were playing a board game because I wanted to distract him from his mom leaving. She would only be gone for an hour or so.

We went inside and Calvin stopped crying. Since it was summertime and broad daylight, I left the front door wide open with just the screen door shut, and there was no lock on the screen door. As Calvin and I played our board game, I heard the loudest voice I've ever heard within me shout "Get up and shut the door!" I couldn't help but listen it was so loud. I immediately got up.

When I approached the door and grabbed the knob to shut it, I saw a station wagon with four or five teenage boys in it pulling up to park on the side of Sue's house. One of the boys had gotten out of the car and was walking up the driveway. This all happened within minutes of my mom and sister leaving.

Who is that? At first I thought it was someone coming to deliver something. Hurriedly, I shut the door and locked it. The kid knocked on the door and asked me to open it because he said he had something for me to look at. He had a clipboard in his hand with a pen in it, as if he were selling something. And he kept asking me if my mother or father were home.

"Yes, they are sleeping!" I shouted in my fearful defense.

"I just saw them leave," the boy responded. In that moment I realized the boys were waiting for my mom and sister to leave so they could make an entrance. I couldn't see clearly through the stained-glass windows on the wooden door. There were three big square windows, and the door was thick. The boys were not leaving.

"I'm calling the cops," I said to Calvin in a low voice. He and I used to play cops and robbers so he thought it was a game. He screamed, "Yeah, call the cops! We're calling the cops!" I later realized it was at that moment that the boys fled. I called 911; Calvin and I ducked into the dining room until the police arrived. One of the officers said those same neighborhood boys had earlier tried to rob another house.

Divine Encounters

God has saved my life so many times. The loud voice that shouted at me from within was Him. I got up at the perfect time to shut that door. If I didn't hear that voice, I never would've gotten up! Calvin and I would've been in danger. God protected us.

My mother used to have a large painting mounted on the brick wall over our fireplace. It was of the Virgin Mary holding baby Jesus with two apostles kneeling at their feet. When I was a child, I would stare at that picture. It was hard to miss because it was right next to the television where I would sit and watch *The Cosby Show* and other sitcoms after school.

My favorite show around that age was *The Cosby Show*. They represented the all-American family. The father, Bill Cosby, was a doctor; the mother, Claire, was an attorney. They had dinner together and through lessons and conversations taught their children about life. I remember wishing I could be in their family. I never experienced that kind of peace.

I remember looking at the picture and studying it during commercial breaks. I always felt the reality of Jesus in my heart, but I had questions. I was confused. Just like the incident of babysitting at eleven when I heard a voice. This time the voice was softer, not so loud and profound.

"*You're going to live forever.*"

What do you mean, God, I'm going to live forever? Nobody lives forever. How could someone live forever? I thought.

Again the voice of the Almighty repeated, "*Zina, you're going to live with Me forever.*"

Forever, God? Really? What does that mean?

It was the love of God professing to me that all the pain I had encountered in my young journey, all the pain I was getting ready to embark upon, had a purpose, a meaning—all the confusion, suffering, and uncertainty. There is no end. For we have a glorious kingdom called heaven awaiting us. I had feelings. I had thoughts.

I remember my friend Melissa calling me one day sobbing, asking me to hurry up and come over to her house. As a good friend, I did. She was scared because another friend, who had just left, told Melissa that she would not go to heaven because her family was Catholic.

Melissa was crying and believed the young girl. I was only twelve, but I explained to Melissa that this was not true. God loved all of us, Christians, Catholics, even non-Christians too. I assured her that she would not go to hell and that the girl was mistaken. Melissa calmed down after our conversation.

I always blamed this accident for being different. I reflect while I write. I realize I've always been different, from a young age. I was mature. Maybe that's why they had me babysitting at eleven. Indeed, the accident changed my life and made me stronger, but at a young age I already had an old soul.

I was the one socializing with the elders at my friends' houses when they just wanted to go upstairs and get away from them and act like teens. That could be why my teachers treated me differently. That could be why I represented the Multicultural/Multiracial Council at Harrison High. That could be why I wanted to be a teacher too.

During college, I would try to fit in and sometimes go to clubs with friends on the weekends. I had fun being in groups, but it was the atmosphere. I heard that still small voice again: *"You're wasting your time here. I have more than this for you."* I couldn't wait to get back to my studies or goals I was currently working on, or do something productive.

I've always enjoyed going to church alone. I can focus. When I take someone with me, I get distracted easily. I've never really had a church home. People sometimes ask me what church I go to. I like a lot of them. I often visit churches of friends when they ask me to go with them. Even though I grew up in a Catholic family, I've gone to non-denominational, Baptist, and Pentecostal churches. One of my favorite pastors to watch on YouTube is Bishop T.D. Jakes. I believe he is a great prophet of our time.

My mother would get upset with me when I missed church on Sundays. She knew that I regularly went to church alone. She would urge me to go, and I used to say to her, "Church is in my heart, Mom. When I miss church, God is still there. He understands." This would frustrate her.

A Teacher of a Different Kind

I went on several women's retreats in my twenties—a few times with my sisters and friends, the other times alone. I requested spiritual counseling once, and they referred me to a priest named Father Dressman. He gave me some really wise instruction one time that I will never forget, on one of my visits at the large retreat house and conference center where he lives. Sadly, he suffers from Alzheimer's disease so he doesn't always remember me anymore. He's ninety-one now. The greatest lesson I learned from him was his humility.

On this one visit, he was extremely intuitive and kept talking about the mystery, the love of Christ, how it surpasses everything and how the love of God that resides in our hearts is the inner peace. There's an inner peace when you know, when you believe, when you walk with the Lord. He says I have that peace, to know Jesus is always here. I am never lonely. He says he knows I've always had that, as he does. And it's the inspiration, the strength that comes from God that He gives us. The ability I have. The gift to teach. It all comes from God.

Father Dressman says not everyone sees it that way, but he does. He knows I do too. "We are to be as vehicles," he said. "Messengers. Workers of service. The inner peace and contentment allows us to see. Nothing else matters. All the tangibles, all the material, all that I see doesn't mean much. I have Christ. I am loved. When we know that, and when we experience that, it provides confidence. And all the little stuff like success, more money, marriage—does not matter much."

He says I was carefully chosen to go through this journey. "Yes, we say by chance. But no, you were selected and chosen. You are a different kind of teacher, more than just English. I think the greatest gift you have to give is your example. That is how we learn. Not always with words but by example. We have people that we call miracle workers, the great miracle workers—you could be one of them." He pointed his finger at me. "You are."

God always told me my path would not be easy. I knew this road would be hard. Whenever I got a chance, I was outside as a child riding my bike. On those nights I remember feeling God's presence strongly. **I was getting instruction on the steps of my life.** There would be some trying times, but I would make it through. God would also tell me that I had something significant to do. I knew other kids were not like me. I used to feel weird for having these feelings and thoughts.

Now I understand. I had a special mission to fulfill, one that God handpicked me to carry out. That doesn't mean it's been easy. I've had struggles, to say the least. Overcoming loneliness, depression, and learning to walk after paralysis were not *where it all began*—and they are not the end of the story either. Writing this book has helped me heal greatly, as I reflect on my faith and am constantly reminded that the Lord is always with me. He is with all of us.

Chapter 9

Where I Am Now

"…For I am the Lord that [continuously] heals you."
Exodus 15:26

If I can help one person through my writing, I am appeased. The more people I can help, the better. The positive reinforcement from my blog has meant so much to me. Though I'm introverted by nature, I've learned to be social and outgoing. I've gotten better at extending myself because since high school I had to learn to make new friends, when my old ones left me. God has blessed me with some wonderful friends.

Still, it is sometimes hard for me to relate to people my age. I grew up different having an accident so young. I grew up with a physical challenge. I grew up with God as my source of everything. Even in my mid-thirties, I feel there are times I cannot relate.

There are still some days when I don't feel so good. Occasional aches and pains from headaches or muscle strain from over-activity is normal for all of us. The only place I still get some nerve pain is in my right leg. I have never had trouble with spasms, where a person's legs move involuntarily, with no warning.

I have a friend who is a quadriplegic that said his legs have even jumped up and kicked him in the face. I know it sounds drastic. I feel blessed that I've only had nerve pain. Now it is so mild and usually near my right ankle and foot.

If I've had a long day I may get some nerve pain, especially if I walk on the treadmill or use the elliptical machine. But it goes away quickly. I may also get a little pain if I'm overly tired, but it's so mild.

God knows my body, of that I am confident. He knows my body better than any world-class doctor or surgeon ever could. After all, He is my creator. My divine healer. My Great Physician. The passage I quoted in the beginning of this chapter says, *"For I am the Lord who [continuously] heals you."* I think that statement is powerful, and the word "continuously" says a lot. It proves that healing has to recur rather than be a onetime event. All of us get sick more than once. Healing may even have to be continuous for the big healing to come. Or we may need to be healed again and again.

I ask God to help me if I feel any discouragement or pain. I lie down. I may take an occasional Tylenol. I don't take any other medications. I sometimes get a feeling that Jesus is touching the area that is causing me pain. I sometimes get headaches, but I get well. Just talking to God helps me. I am releasing the pain.

I have been blessed to get on my feet through a lot of hard work, prayer, and faith. I've completed a ton of physical therapy. It takes that. If you don't put in the time and effort, if you just accept your condition, you may not get better. I have seen it happen before, and it is a great tragedy. I think most of all you have to believe in Him, but you also have to do the work. It takes determination. It takes stamina. It takes patience.

I have never believed that I could make all this progress on my own, with my own capabilities. I am determined. I am motivated, but I know I have a God who loves me, who has allowed me to do those things. Like get up in front of a classroom and teach from crutches. Or walk into the Nissan Technical Center. People wonder what is wrong with me. I am in the game, but I am not the same. I don't look like them. They look out of curiosity. It is clear there was something I had to overcome.

How did I get here? It took faith. I wrote this book to share how I learned to walk again. How I was able to get through college and earn two degrees. How I have a successful teaching career. How I'm independent and able to take care of myself.

I pray that those of you facing similar circumstances of spinal cord injury will read my words and gain some insight. I pray that those who are suffering in any way will be inspired.

Spinal cord injury has shaped the last half of my life. There is no way I would have gotten through the major obstacles without the Lord. In the first moments that I was aware of my surroundings after the accident, to the first hours and the first days, I looked to God. Without my faith, without Jesus, I never would've been able to get through any of it.

I'm grateful that He's always been in my life leading me and guiding me. Writing this memoir has allowed me to see how much God has helped me. I hope you see how much He can help you. Writing this book has been healing for me. I hope it can be healing for you.

In the Gospel of Matthew (9:1-8), Jesus heals a paralytic:

> Then behold they brought to Him a paralytic lying on a bed. When Jesus saw their faith, He said to the paralytic, "Son, be of good cheer; your sins are forgiven you." And at once some of the scribes said within themselves, "This Man blasphemes!" But Jesus, knowing their thoughts, said, "Why do you think evil in your hearts? For which is easier, to say, 'Your sins are forgiven you,' or to say, 'Arise and walk?' But that you may know that the Son of Man has power on earth to forgive sins" – then He said to the paralytic, "Arise, take up your bed, and go to your house." And he arose and departed to his house. Now when the multitudes saw it, they marveled and glorified God, who had given such power to men.

John 5 contains another story of a paralytic being healed by the pool at Bethesda. For thirty-eight years that man lay crippled, waiting for a miracle. When Jesus sees him, He looks down with compassion and asks a pointed yet poignant question: "Do you want to be well?"

A woman from Australia wrote to me a few times on my blog asking if we could Skype. She had some questions. I agreed, so we did. After a few minutes of introduction, she began. I answered all her questions as best I could.

Midway into our conversation she said, "So much for the story," in reference to this story from the Gospel of Matthew about a paralytic being healed. She was being sarcastic and suggesting that it could not be true, because she still has paralysis and I still have some trouble walking too. I reminded her that the man by the pool at Bethesda waited thirty-eight years. It was like a light bulb went off in her head and she smiled and said, "Yes, that is true."

Why does spinal cord injury take so much from us? Why does it take so long to recover when Jesus easily healed this paralytic man? Why is it so hard for us to just get up and walk?

One thing I couldn't help but notice as I read this story over and over several times is that first Jesus had to forgive the man's sins, and then he was able to get up and walk. Jesus says, "Son, be of good cheer; your sins are forgiven you." When the scribes and Pharisees challenge Jesus, thinking He lied, He says, "For which is easier, to say, 'Your sins are forgiven you,' or to say, 'Arise and walk?' But that you may know that the Son of Man has power on earth to forgive sins—" Then the man gets up and walks.

This tells me there is a direct connection between sin and healing. A personal sin is a free and informed choice to reject God's law, according to Father Jonathan Morris in *The Promise: God's Purpose and Plan for When Life Hurts*. The effect of sin, in my life, in all our lives, can deprive us, hold us back. I believe it can keep us sick or make us sick.

I once heard a pastor say that sin is anything that separates us from the love of Christ. If someone harms themselves by smoking excessively or drinking too much, that is self-destructive. Is that not sin? When we are destroying ourselves, how can we heal—in any form? When we are living right and doing our best, it reflects on the outside.

These passages are very symbolic. When Jesus lifted the burden of sin from the man, the man was able to walk. The miracle is that Jesus is the one able to heal our sin, and we are all guilty of it. Not only did the man get healed and walk again, but he was freed from sin—the greatest miracle.

When we choose to live right, we can heal more because we are healing ourselves. When we become well on the inside, we can become well on the outside too.

I speak here from my own experience. I am in no way claiming that everyone would just get up and walk after spinal cord injury if only they had faith and never did anything wrong. Sadly, some people gain little recovery or don't recover at all. I can't even begin to claim I know why some heal and others don't. But I know we have to try. If we never try to get well, be well with ourselves by living right, how will we recover and heal from anything, whether it be a personal problem or spinal cord injury? We have to do good for ourselves. We have to try!

A Blessed Reunion

Throughout the process of writing this book over the last couple of years, details and memories floated back to me. For example, I was convinced that Mary Kay was an angel. When I recalled her presence on the helicopter ride and remembered her voice,

I wondered, *God, was she real?* I thought she may have been a celestial angel that God sent in those moments to save my life.

In October 2011, while I was writing my book, I met my good friend Ginger and her friend Rich out at dinner one evening. Rich was a fireman, and Ginger knew that I had been recalling events and still had some unanswered questions. All the information in this book is accurate since I have pulled medical and even police reports.

Ginger had wanted me to meet Rich for some time because she thought it might help me, that maybe he could answer any additional questions since his job is to save people in emergency situations. I asked him a lot of questions. I wanted to know more about exactly what happened to me. Rich kindly explained the danger when I recalled the events, and he told me how lucky I was.

I was still puzzled by the woman on the helicopter though and whether or not she was real, so I talked with Ginger and Rich about it. Many painful memories that I had blocked for so long came back to me while writing this book. I have shed a few tears in the process of writing. Good tears. Tears of pain. Tears of release. Tears of letting go. Specifically, I was praying for the truth about the woman on the helicopter, Mary Kay, who kept me alive.

At dinner, Ginger and Rich invited me to an upcoming Bloomfield Hills Township firemen's open house that was coming up. Ginger really wanted me to attend because she knew it would be helpful. She said a U of M Survival Life Flight helicopter would also be there on display for the parents and children to see. Some of the U of M staff would be on hand to talk with the parents and children.

So I went. I saw the helicopter as soon as I parked my car. I called Ginger on my cell phone and she told me to just start walking up to it; she would meet me outside.

There was a woman standing by the helicopter, not too tall, blonde hair, semi-curled. Maybe in her late forties or early fifties. She turned to look at me as I walked up. I couldn't help but notice her eyes. Right away I recognized her but I couldn't recall from where. I knew I had seen her before. Her eyes were distinct—a striking light blue that ran deep. Ginger told me to start asking her questions so I did. First the woman showed me the helicopter, and soon after I told her of my accident.

Although I thought I was meeting a stranger, it felt like I was not seeing her for the first time. I told her my name and asked if she had heard about my accident. The first thing she said was, "You were on your way to school."

I told her it was in October of 1994.

"Yeah, I was with you," she responded, surprised but very certain it was me. I told her I remembered her eyes.

"Your abdomen," she said as her voice got lower. "I remember you by your abdomen because I had never seen anything like it before." She has been a flight nurse for about twenty-five years.

We hugged. I thanked her for playing a major role in saving my life. She told me how proud she was of me. We kept in contact through email, even by telephone. Her details added some information to chapter one of this book. She explained that the University of Michigan hospital is a level-one trauma center for teens and adults and that taking me there "was the best thing that could've happened for you."

Love is powerful. It has the power to heal and the power to save. The love that came from Mary Kay, the love that came from everyone at Mott Children's Hospital immediately following that day, the love that came from my family and friends, the love that came from my teachers and principals when I went back to school—**love is what kept me alive in the most critical of times**.

There is still not enough we can do about spinal cord injury. We are told there is yet to be a cure. But we have to have *faith*. A glimmer of hope…a light in the darkness…in what seems to be hopeless…peace of mind in crisis…and we have to have love.

"And now abide faith, hope, and love, these three; but the greatest of these is love" (Corinthians 13:13).

About the Author

Zina Hermez is an author, teacher, and native of the metro Detroit area. She writes articles on faith and overcoming disability. Her story has been featured in *Christianity Today* and *Spinal Cord Injury Zone*. She has written articles for non-profits, healthcare, and various other publications. An educator for over ten years, she has taught multiple subjects to hundreds of students of all ages, from many different backgrounds and cultures. Today she is an instructor of English for a global language training company and also does classroom teaching.

Zina holds a B.A. in English with a minor in history from Oakland University in Rochester Hills, Michigan. She is an active member of writer's groups both off-line and online. When Zina is not writing or teaching, she enjoys spending time with family, listening to music, exercising, and being social with friends. Her website can be found at www.zinahermez.com.

Appendix 1

What Do the Doctors Say?

The University of Alabama at Birmingham Spinal Cord Injury Model System (UAB-SCIMS) answered questions about the latest cutting-edge research done on stem-cell surgery to cure the spinal cord in June 2013. The UAB-SCIMS is one of only fourteen spinal cord injury (SCI) model systems in the United States. When asked how far we are from getting a cure through stem-cell research they answered:

> The term "stem cell" is a broad one that includes many types of cells from many different tissue origins. Although current advances in stem cell research and technology show that stem cells **may** have therapeutic potential, many unanswered questions remain and

other new questions emerge. For example, each type of stem cell has specific attributes and it is not yet known which cell type is the "best" for repair after SCI. Also, questions of what dose (i.e. how many cells and what time after SCI) and safety in humans have not yet been answered in clinical trials. Thus, more research is vital to understanding the potential and application of this promising approach. It is an exciting time for stem cell research, but many crucial questions about the use of stem cells remain. As there are many features of the use of stem cell transplant therapy that remain unknown, it is impossible to provide a definitive timeline. Important research progress continues to be made but too many unknown variables remain for a time-line to cure to be laid out.

In a desperate attempt to walk again, patients sometimes turn to alternative options such as stem-cell surgery. Adult stem cells are extracted from other parts of the body and implanted into the spinal cord at the site of injury. The surgery does not solve the problem. As noted, there is no guarantee that it will be the cure. "The most important thing we've learned is that surgery is not enough. It has to be accompanied by rehabilitation (exercise)," says Dr. Carlos Lima, a neuron-pathologist on the Lisbon stem-cell team.

For those reasons, I'm glad I never wanted to experiment with having stem-cell surgery. God, faith, and prayer have always been my remedies. I believe it would have held me back in making progress or, even worse, harmed me. I have heard adverse stories about people who had stem-cell surgery. I've also heard stories of people who remained neutral or got very little return.

The nervous system controls everything in your body. The true extent of many injuries isn't fully known until six to eight weeks post-injury. The spinal cord normally goes into what is called spinal shock after it has been damaged. The swelling and fluid masses showing on any resultant X-ray, MRI, or CT scans may well mask the true nature of the underlying injury.

We have now come out with Ekso Bionics, the first of its kind out of Berkeley, California, founded in 2010. Ekso Bionics are eLEGS, an intelligent, bionic exoskeleton that actually allows wheelchair users to stand and walk over ground. These were initially used for soldiers carrying heavy cargo while going uphill. The solid legs and back helped them prevent injury. The problem is the device weighs 50 pounds, and adding that much weight I don't know how functional you can be. Or how much time you can spend on them during the day.

The latest form of eLEGS is ReWalk, another battery-powered robotic exoskeleton. The ReWalk exoskeleton allows an ambulation and rehabilitation alternative to wheelchair users, enabling people with paraplegia and other types of lower-limb dysfunction to stand, walk, and climb stairs.

Dr. Jeffrey Rosenbluth, the medical director of the Spinal Cord Injury Acute Rehabilitation program at the University of Utah Health Sciences Center, described the device: "You're looking at the ReWalk exoskeleton," he said. "It's a wearable robotic device that enables folks with spinal cord injuries, and limited or no use of their lower extremities, to actually walk, to get out of their wheelchair, and to actually walk!"

Mary, a twenty-four-year-old with a T10 spinal cord injury, uses the system and says when you first get into it, it is uncomfortable. "When the machine stands, it does so rather quickly and thus abruptly stretches all the muscles that tighten while sitting, so it is not so comfortable. It is not a machine that you just strap into and it walks for you; there is a large learning curve to ascend while perfecting the weight shifts and body positioning."

Mary likes it because she sees herself walking for social outings with friends or, for example, going to the park or walking around an art fair in the future. She likes the technology but finds it exciting to think of how much better a lighter weight and smarter ReWalk could be for everyday use in place of a wheelchair.

I complete studies with the University of Michigan Spinal Cord Injury Model System (UM-SCIMS) at least a few times a year. The UM-SCIMS is one of the fourteen SCI model systems in the United States, including the University of Alabama at Birmingham Spinal Cord Injury Model System (UAB-SCIMS.)

Successfully funded since 1985, UM-SCIMS works to regularly keep in touch with those interested in being a part of the SCI model systems, to monitor clinical issues and collect key information to conduct research. Their goal is to enhance care. I always gladly cooperate when they ask me to complete a study. It pays little, but it's not the money that drives me to do it. It's helping the University of Michigan in any way I can, because that is the hospital that saved my life!

On one of our telephone interviews, they proudly told me that the ReWalk system has now been approved by the FDA for use within rehabilitation centers in the United States. And that the University of Michigan would be the first rehabilitation site in the Midwest to have the ReWalk. A home unit, designed for personal use, is currently undergoing FDA approval and is expected to be available in 2014. Like Ekso Bionics, the ReWalk has a heavy back that appears to be a backpack.

I'm grateful I don't need the ReWalk or Ekso Bionics to walk, but for this advancement I am very thankful because I think it will change lives for the better and help a lot of people to walk. Even if minimally, it will get them out of their wheelchairs. I've always looked to God and my faith, and since I know He is capable of doing anything above and beyond our imagination, I know that all healing comes from Him.

I believe it is never too late to heal from SCI naturally, without technology or assistive walking devices. I never believed the adage that I would get the most out of my recovery only two years after my accident. That could be why I am still making progress. It requires effort and lots of work. In 2 Corinthians 12:9, Jesus says, "My grace is sufficient for you, for *my* power is made perfect in weakness." I have felt that. I have been given strength in the times when I felt the most weak—both physically and spiritually.

I can't explain how much gratitude I have for God in my heart. My life is a miracle, and so is the ability to walk. No one can understand how freeing it is unless they've gone from paralyzed to walking. I held onto what He told me. I would walk. I did. Still not exactly as well as I would like. But I do not plan on giving up.

Startling Facts about Spinal Cord Injury

One in five Americans is disabled, according to the United States Census Bureau. Disability takes a toll on those affected and their families. It can rob an individual of their quality of life. Especially if you're young, in my opinion it's more detrimental. It affects the use of your body, your emotions, your self-esteem, and your overall quality of life.

Spinal cord injury (SCI) is one form of disability, and it causes paralysis, pain, shortness of breath, involuntary muscle spasms, discomfort, and emotional stress, to name just a few of the side effects. It can even put someone on a ventilator, depending upon their level of injury.

SCI refers to any injury to the spinal cord that is caused by trauma instead of disease. Depending on where the spinal cord and nerve roots are damaged, the symptoms can vary, but in nearly every case it causes someone to be paralyzed.

Motor vehicle accidents account for 39 percent of all spinal cord injuries, falls 28 percent, acts of violence 15 percent, sporting activities 8 percent, and other unknown 10 percent according to the Mike Utley Foundation. The annual incidence of SCI not including those who die at the scene of the accident is approximately twelve thousand new cases each year.

Some statistics show that only 300,000 people live with a spinal cord injury in the US alone, but I had a feeling that number was much higher. I was right. According to an article that recognized Spinal Cord Injury Awareness Month by the Christopher and Dana Reeve Foundation as of September 3, 2013, "More than 5.6 million Americans, or one in 50 people, live with some form of paralysis. Of those, 1.275 million are living with paralysis due to a spinal cord injury." Some 40 percent of all SCIs result in quadriplegia (paralysis of all four limbs), and 60 percent in paraplegia (paralysis of lower extremities), according to the Spinal Injuries Association.

The medical field offers *little hope* for recovery. Doctors say only 0 to 2 percent of people with spinal cord injuries walk again.

A study was done on 142 people with paraplegia, one year after their injury. The findings were: less than half, 38 percent, of the studied subjects had any sort of recovery. Out of those, only 5 percent recovered enough function to walk, and they required crutches and other assistive devices. All of them had injuries below T11. Of those 5 percent, only 4 percent of that population was considered "incomplete" spinal cord injuries—meaning they had some return of muscles and function, according to Wikipedia.com.

The trauma is not only physical, it's psychological. There can be loss of friendships, abandonment, relationship break-ups, rejection, and even marital separation and divorce. When struck with paralysis, an individual initially feels shock, confusion, and disbelief. *What will life be like in a wheelchair?* they ponder. They may feel numb emotionally. It doesn't completely register and they feel uncertainty.

The Cost of Being Injured

The person's financial state is also compromised. What if the person is injured and has no health insurance? This is too often the case. What if they were not covered by auto insurance and the accident wasn't vehicle-related? What if they simply fell? What if they were hurt in a sporting accident? Who will cover all of the physical therapy, doctors, and rehabilitation appointments?

Lifetime costs for a spinal-cord-injured person range from $1 million to $5 million, depending upon the level of injury.

For those with higher-level injuries requiring power wheelchairs and around-the-clock assistance, it could be even more. I've heard of cases where the costs were $1 million per year! This is not unheard of.

The higher the level of injury, the higher the cost because of the dependency on nurses, doctors, home-health aides, and overall assistance. People with traumatic brain injury (TBI) may require more help. This financial hardship creates just another burden to bear.

People hold fundraisers to gather money if they are not insured, but it rarely solves the problem. Unless you are a millionaire, you cannot afford to get injured. What do you do when life becomes unpredictable? Who do you turn to? Even if victims receive some sort of government or state compensation, it is not enough to cover the high costs of healthcare. This stress can cause a downward spiral in the individual's health if they are not getting enough exercise, enough movement—their health can be compromised quickly.

For someone with SCI, it's not enough to have a limited amount of physical therapy sessions per year. In order to recover or walk, the patient typically needs an unlimited number of hours of physical therapy.

ASIA Classifications

Doctors say the spinal cord is a very complex organ. After all, in combination with the brain, it controls every single aspect of our body. Hence, when the spinal cord sustains damage people lose more than just the ability to walk—they can even lose the usage of their arms.

Aside from the loss of movement and sensation, depending on where in the spinal cord the injury occurs, there may be additional impairments such as the loss of finger movement, the ability to grasp things, and the ability to feel the toes.

There is a lot that we don't know about SCI. Hospitals conduct studies. The University of Michigan Spinal Cord Injury Model System (UM-SCIMS) is one of the SCI model systems in the United States. They call me periodically to complete studies.

Sometimes nerves and muscles are supposed to be damaged below the level of a spinal break, and the patient gets some return and they heal. Doctors may deem the person's injury as "incomplete." Spinal cord injuries are described at various levels which can vary from having no effect on the patient to a "complete" injury, meaning a total loss of function.

The American Spinal Injury Association (ASIA) first published an international classification of spinal cord injury in 1982, called the *International Standards for Neurological and Functional Classification of Spinal Cord Injury*. There are five categories:

- A indicates a "complete" spinal cord injury where no motor or sensory function is preserved in the sacral segments of S4 and S5.
- B indicates an "incomplete" spinal cord injury where sensory but not motor function is preserved below the neurological level and includes the sacral segments of S4-S5.
- C indicates an "incomplete" spinal cord injury where motor function is preserved below the neurological level and more than half of key muscles below the neurological level have a muscle grade of less than 3.
- D indicates an "incomplete" spinal cord injury where motor function is preserved below the neurological level and at least half of the key muscles below the neurological level have a muscle grade of 3 or more.
- E indicates "normal" motor and sensory function.

Dr. Deschpande, my rehabilitation doctor, said I am at a D classification. This is a good grade!

Research into treatments for SCI include controlled hypothermia and stem cells, though many treatments have not been studied thoroughly and very little new research has been implemented in standard care.

Patrick Rummerfield is the first fully functioning quadriplegic in the world. He learned to walk again without the assistance of any walking device. He doesn't have a limp when he walks. He is not a paraplegic he is a quadriplegic, which makes walking that much harder, because he initially lost the usage of all four limbs.

Oftentimes people who have injuries at a lower level do not see that much progress. Again, there is still a lot we don't know about SCI. Studies don't give us all the answers. Why do some people heal when others remain wheelchair-confined? Is it an issue of not putting in enough effort? Not using enough energy? Not having enough faith? I believe you need all of those components. Effort, energy, and faith; number one, it starts with you. *It has to start with you!*

CPSIA information can be obtained at www.ICGtesting.com
Printed in the USA
LVOW07s1826171014

409312LV00003B/99/P